THE TANCOOK WHALERS
Origins, Rediscovery, and Revival

THE TANCOOK WHALERS
Origins, Rediscovery, and Revival

Robert C. Post

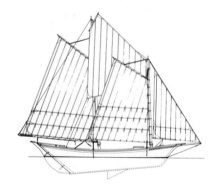

Bath, Maine
Maine Maritime Museum
1985

This publication is made possible with funds
from the
National Endowment for the Arts
NEA 02-5330-040
and the
National Trust for Historic Preservation
Maritime Division

Library of Congress Catalog
Card Number 85-63457
ISBN 0-937410-05-5

Composition and production by
Post Scripts, East Boothbay, Maine

Design by Diana Eames Esterly

Printed in the United States of America by
Nimrod Press, Boston, Massachusetts

Cover: The *Vernon Langille,* the Tancook whaler completed in 1979
by the Maine Maritime Museum's Apprenticeshop, beats into a
smoky Sou'wester. Photograph by Diana Eames Esterly

TO THE MEMORY OF
VERNON LANGILLE

Vernon Langille, boatbuilder of Tancook Island,
in 1913 at age 25. Maritime Museum of the
Atlantic (MMA), Halifax, Nova Scotia

Contents

Foreword

Isn't there a subtle psychic connection between islands and double-ended boats? I think perhaps there is. Boats that serve islands, all around the world, seem to be predominantly double-enders. Maybe it's something about the very environment of an island that suggests to an islander that his boat should be pointed at both ends. Maybe it's that a double-ender often gives a great sense of seaworthiness and that the islander knows that he may want to get ashore onto the main on any day of reasonable hard weather—and may need to on some day of unreasonable weather.

At any rate, double-ended island boats make a fascinating study, and none more so than those of the coastal islands of New England and Nova Scotia. Far and away the prettiest of all these craft is the Tancook whaler, the schooner-rigged double-ender that served Tancook Islanders in Mahone Bay, Nova Scotia. These are fine, able vessels that well met all the watery needs of the Tancook Islanders; unlike some of their southern counterparts such as the seaworthy pinkies and Block Island boats, the Tancook whalers were fast, sailing much like a pre-World War II racing yacht, except for speed to windward.

Such a refined type of traditional vessel deserves emulation, and, happily, through the years since the last Tancook whaler worked under sail, a number of fine copies of them, as well as some sensible, modified versions, have been built and sailed. It is good to perpetuate such nicely-developed craft, for their working life was a mere half-century. Nor were there more than something like fifty Tancook whalers sailing at any one time.

I count myself extremely lucky to have been able to spend a fair bit of time sailing in the *Vernon Langille,* the excellent Tancook-whaler replica built by the Apprenticeshop of the Maine Maritime Museum, and to have been the proud owner of a fine little twenty-five-foot Tancook-whaler replica. These boats were certainly as much fun to sail as any; they never disturbed the water much as they slipped smoothly along, but rather caused stirs of admiration wherever they went.

I can't decide what I like best about Tancook whalers; the fact that they served an island people so well, or their sharp, hollow, clipper bows, or their dainty wine-glass sections, or their well-raked, pointed sterns, or maybe their overlapping workhorse foresails. Anyway, the Tancook whaler is all of a piece, and she's absolutely elegant.

Scraps of information have been published here and there about the Tancook whaler, but this is the first chance they've had for a whole book to themselves. About time, I say.

This book was begun by Lance Lee when he was director of the Maine Maritime Museum's Apprenticeshop. Lance got interested in Tancook whalers through his family; his father and his uncle, William and Derek Lee, had purchased a Tancook whaler named *Evangeline* in 1927. Then William built a Tancook whaler, the *Wind Dog,* in his Harwichport, Massachusetts, boatshop. This exposure gave Lance a big interest in Tancook whalers, and he collected much material on the type while at the Museum. The Tancook archive was left behind as part of the Museum's small-craft Technology Bank when Lance went to begin the Rockport Apprenticeshop. The Museum's new director, John Carter, recognized the value of the project, saw to its continuation, and caused it to result in this book.

The book does a good job of pulling together most of the essential information now known about the Tancook whaler. It probably comes somewhere near the last word on the subject, for it is not very likely that, at this late date, significant new information about the type will be discovered. That said, it should nevertheless be obvious that every- one connected with this project would be delighted if it serves as a magnet to draw forth further tidbits of information about these great boats. For the book is inextricably tied up with the very principle of apprenticing: Passing information and skill from old to young so that an important heritage may live on.

Roger C. Taylor
President, International Marine Publishing Co.

Preface

The Tancook whaler is a particularly handsome vessel. Sleek and graceful, with fine lines, a strong sheer, and a schooner rig, it is well deserving of a second look. But it is deserving for other reasons as well. This publication recounts what is known about the type in general, and what was learned in the process of building a thirty-four-foot Tancook whaler—the *Vernon Langille*—at the Maine Maritime Museum's Apprenticeshop in 1978-79 and sailing her for several years afterward. During that period a wealth of information on regional maritime traditions was compiled by the Museum staff, and the final result is this book by Bob Post.

Credit for building the *Vernon Langille* and for initiating this publication goes to Lance Lee, the founder and first director of the Apprenticeshop. Credit is also due to Dave Foster, master boatbuilder and instructor, and to apprentices Joe Postich and Mark Swanson, who did most of the actual work. The Langille and Stevens families, along with other residents of the Mahone Bay region of Nova Scotia, spent hours and days recounting the oral traditions of Tancook Island and its whalers, and some of them generously loaned or donated plans, photographs, and models. Neils Jannasch and David Fleming of the Maritime Museum of the Atlantic in Halifax searched archives and provided invaluable assistance, as did L.B. Jenson of Hubbards, Nova Scotia. Jim Brown, associate editor of *Down East* magazine, began the initial draft of the manuscript, working from transcriptions of interviews and other material pulled together while he was on the staff of the Museum. Eventually two other staff members, Will Ansel and myself, worked on the project as well. Illustrations were provided by Sam F. Manning, Doug Alvord, and David Dillion.

The staff of the Folk Arts Division of the National Endowment for the Arts, under Bess Lomax Hawes, was consistently supportive. An initial NEA grant helped fund construction of the Apprenticeshop's Tancook whaler as a means of enhancing our knowledge of the arts of traditional wooden boatbuilding, arts which flourished in a great many coastal communities during the 19th century. A second NEA grant helped fund this book as a means of imparting what we had learned. Walter T. Tower, Jr., President of the Nimrod Press, donated toward the book's production.

The *Vernon Langille* was used extensively for sail training and freighting on the Maine coast and beyond until 1983 when she was sold, the proceeds going to fund construction of another traditional schooner, a Maine pinky built on an 1832 model. That project is now nearing completion by the Apprenticeshop. And so the process continues.

Traditional attitudes and traditional values are of crucial importance to an institution such as the Maine Maritime Museum which seeks to interpret a regional seafaring heritage. Hence one of the Museum's primary aims is to preserve an understanding of intangible cultural expressions, expressions such as skill and craftsmanship. In the experience of building and sailing the *Vernon Langille* and in the book which developed out of that experience we have prime examples of the new ways by which museums can communicate with the public.

John S. Carter
Director, Maine Maritime Museum

PROLOGUE

"Damn Good Boats"

A burdensome, wall-sided Tancook whaler with a foreboom.

In February 1933, *Yachting* published an article by Ernest A. Bell titled "The Passing of the Tancook Whaler." The title was a play on words, for Bell wrote about "passing" in two senses. His subject was "a type once popular in the Nova Scotia shore fishery" which was then just about extinct. But he commenced by recounting a tale that was literally about a whaler passing. Some twenty years before, Bell had been bound for Halifax aboard a little coasting steamer. "It was blowing half a gale, and 't'ick-a-fog,' and the skipper had shut her down to see if he could not catch sight or sound of Pennant Whistler." To the starboard came the sound of a conch shell, and a "greasy and perspiring individual" leaning out a half-door to the engine room ventured that it emanated from a fishing boat. Bell went on:

"Shortly, through the fog, appeared brown sails (their sails were nearly always tanned) and a white hull, between 40 and 50 feet long. The boat seemed to approach slowly, to hesitate a moment, and then to leap past in the manner of boats passing at sea—a phenomenon of which Conrad remarks in 'Chance.' But there was time to observe two or three men in yellow oilskins, the helmsman standing with the end of the great ten-foot tiller behind his back, lifted slightly from the comb, and the load of barrels and boxes partly covered by a tarpaulin or, more likely, by the brown staysail (it was not set) in her waist. The man with the shell waved his hand to my friend, who acknowledged the salute graciously. They were then close aboard. The tiller was swung a trifle to weather; the loose-footed overlapping foresail filled with an audible snap, and away she went, at eight or nine knots, her lee rail occasionally awash, and with a smoothness and lack of fuss in that broken water which, somehow, no other boat has ever seemed to me quite able to obtain—and I have known some good ones! . . .

A Tancook whaler at Peggy's Cove, Nova Scotia, in the 1920s.
Maritime Museum of the Atlantic (MMA), Halifax, Nova Scotia

"My friend of the lubrication and perspiration remarked, ere he disappeared below, possibly in answer to a jangle of bells, 'The three Baker boys! Damn good boats, them Tancook whalers!' "

Some two decades later, when David Cabot published an article in the *American Neptune* on "The New England Double Enders," he remarked that Bell's account with the "Damn good boats" yarn remained the only information available on the Tancook whaler. Cabot, however, had written this just prior to publication of Howard I. Chapelle's *American Small Sailing Craft,* which included six pages on the Tancook whaler, with drawings from the lines Chapelle had taken off a hull found at Middle River on Mahone Bay in 1948. Chapelle had illustrated Bell's article, too, his drawings taken from a model made in 1931 by Amos Stevens, whom Bell identified as "the old master builder of Tancook . . . everywhere acknowledged to be the greatest authority on the type, and more responsible for the development of the whaler than any other man." There was a sail plan as well, traced by Chapelle from a drawing by Randolph Stevens, Amos Stevens's son.

Several builder's models of Tancook whalers are extant today, along with the Chapelle drawings and drawings made for the Historic American Merchant Marine Survey (WPA) in the 1930s by W.P. Barnes. And a number of pleasure boats are afloat that have been patterned with some degree of fidelity on the lines of the Tancook whaler—readers of *WoodenBoat* and *National Fisherman* will know of these. Yet the literature on the original Tancook Island workboats has not grown much in more than thirty years. This book, then, seeks to add to that store of information, and also to put the Tancook whaler in the context of life on Tancook Island. The opening section is based on extensive interviews with residents of the island and especially with former residents now living nearby on the mainland who are descended from the men who built and sailed whalers in their heyday.

The succeeding narrative deals with the perpetuation of the Tancook whaler's lines, after it had been superseded in the Nova Scotia shore fishery, by builders on Mahone Bay and in the United States. And, in particular, it provides a first-hand account of a boat built at the Maine Maritime Museum in a manner closely imitative of the way the traditional Tancook Island boatbuilders worked—a boat launched in 1979 and named *Vernon Langille,* after the grandson of Alfred Langille, who built the first whaler on Tancook and who ranks with Amos Stevens for his role in the development of its design.

1 "What a Boat Ought to Look Like"

Isle of Shoals shay from a painting by Arthur Quartley.
Peabody Museum of Salem, Mark Sexton photograph

A sharp, double-ended, schooner-rigged workboat, twenty-five to fifty feet in length with a plank keel and boiler-plate centerboard, the Tancook whaler was developed in the latter half of the 19th century and was superseded about the time of World War I. As with many traditional designs, its origins are vague. It may be that the first builders chose the configuration because, as one veteran observed, "that was their notion of what a boat ought to look like." We do know that it was not uncommon in earlier times for boatbuilders to erect a stem and sternpost on a keel, set a mold roughly amidships, and then plank up from there by eye, lapping the strakes, perhaps with a couple of molds which they moved forward or aft as suited. They would modify subsequent boats to improve sailing characteristics and adapt to local requirements until they had something fully functional.

But the history of technology teaches us that the diffusion of design concepts is as important as their independent origin. Howard Chapelle has thoroughly documented the early interest among the English-speaking colonists of North America in hull forms showing a good turn of speed under sail. He attributes this, in turn, to the interest in profitable but illegal forms of trade and to chronically unstable international relations. From the late 17th century to the 19th, there was a succession of vessel types that embodied design characteristics conducive to speed, characteristics that are also found in the Tancook whaler. Take, for example, a British Admiralty Draught in the archives of the National Maritime Museum at Greenwich of an American-built sloop of 1741 called *Mediator*. The plan shows a vessel that is double-ended on the waterline (although it has an overhanging pierced transom), with a beam-to-length ratio of a little better than one to three. There is a good bit of drag to the keel, and a rising floor in the midsection with hollow garboards and likewise a hollow entrance forward. To be sure, striking dissimilarities exist between this apple-bowed colonial sloop and the slim-waisted Tancook whalers, but what is important to note is that by the mid-18th century the formula for a fast, able sailing vessel was well understood by builders on Chesapeake Bay, where *Mediator* came from. It would not have taken long for knowledge of this formula to diffuse widely to builders elsewhere on the Atlantic Coast who would adapt its features to local conditions and the tasks at hand.

One of the earliest small American double-enders was the whaleboat, dating to the middle or even early 18th century. Initially worked from shore, these were soon put aboard larger vessels in pursuit of migrating whales. Whaleboats were generally constructed of cedar planking, both lapstrake and smooth (or combination), over wide, steam-bent oak frames which were often tapered. They had hard bilges, hollow floors, fine ends, a raking bow and stern, and a beam-to-length ratio as high as one to five. Weight was given careful consideration as the boats had to be hauled ashore or aboard. There is little doubt that whaleboats were in evidence along the coast of Nova Scotia during the early part of the 19th century.

A more distinct type of double-ender that evolved from the earlier square-sterned shallops was the New England boat in its many variations. Most were two-masters used in shore fisheries. Chapelle, after recording the lines of the derelict hull he found at Middle River in 1948, speculated that the Tancook whaler could have derived from a small, schooner-rigged, shallow-draft type thought to have originated in the area of Hampton-Seabrook, New Hampshire, around 1805. These Hampton boats were maneuverable—smart sailers used to fish the coastal ledges as well as offshore—and apparently they changed little between the 1830s and 1880s. In 1936 Chapelle recorded the lines from one found in a marsh near York, Maine, which was thought to date from the 1880s. Recorded data is nonexistent, however, and what has been written about the Hampton boat is largely speculative. Besides, Chapelle writes, "there were really two distinct types of [Hampton] boats, each having two variations or subtypes. . . . This has led to confusion in the attempts to trace the development of the type, and its history has become clouded by conflicting local claims. . . ."

The other distinct type was a Maine Hampton boat whose bow in fact resembled that of a Tancook whaler more closely than did that of the New Hampshire variety. Local sources claim this Maine variation had an independent inception at Harpswell or Bailey's Island.

An account exists that places boats of a Hampton type off the coast of British North America as early as 1833. Describing the Labrador cod fishery in his *Delineations of American Scenery and Character*, John J. Audubon wrote:

"A vessel of one hundred tons or so is provided with a crew of twelve men, who are equally expert as sailors or fishers, and for every couple of these hardy tars a Hampton boat is provided . . . at three in the morning the crew are prepared for their days labour and ready to betake themselves to their boats, each of which has two oars and lugsails."

The Fisheries and Fishery Industries of the United States, George Brown Goode's masterwork which remains largely definitive though nearly a century old, indicates that the Labrador schooners sailing out of Massachusetts and Maine ports "always carried four or five boats of the pattern now generally known as the 'Hampton' boat, but around Newburyport still known as the 'Labrador' boat." Goode notes that these were lapstraked, averaged about nineteen feet on keel and twenty-three overall, and were very sharp forward and aft with a straight sternpost. Generally two-masters rigged with sprit or leg-o'-mutton sails, they were stowed on deck, two to a side, and swung on stern davits. And they were often called whalers—by the 19th century the term seems to have been applied generically to any small double-ender.

After a season's fishing, skippers of Grand Banks schooners often put in at ports along the way home and sold their smaller boats to local fishermen. Certainly they could have visited Halifax, and indeed one Tancook old-timer did recall seeing a "Labrador whaler" on the island when he was young. It seems reasonable to assume that if an imported type performed well for the islanders, they would have copied aspects of its design. A vessel found at St. Pierre, Quebec, whose lines Chapelle took off in 1952, and which he identified rather enigmatically as an "English coast type," is interesting in that it seems to be a transitional craft between the Hampton, Labrador, and Tancook whalers. It approximates the Hampton construction with its full keel and clenched lapped planking. Like the Hampton boat, it has a moderate run aft, but it is roughly ten feet longer. It also shows the raking sternpost and flattened

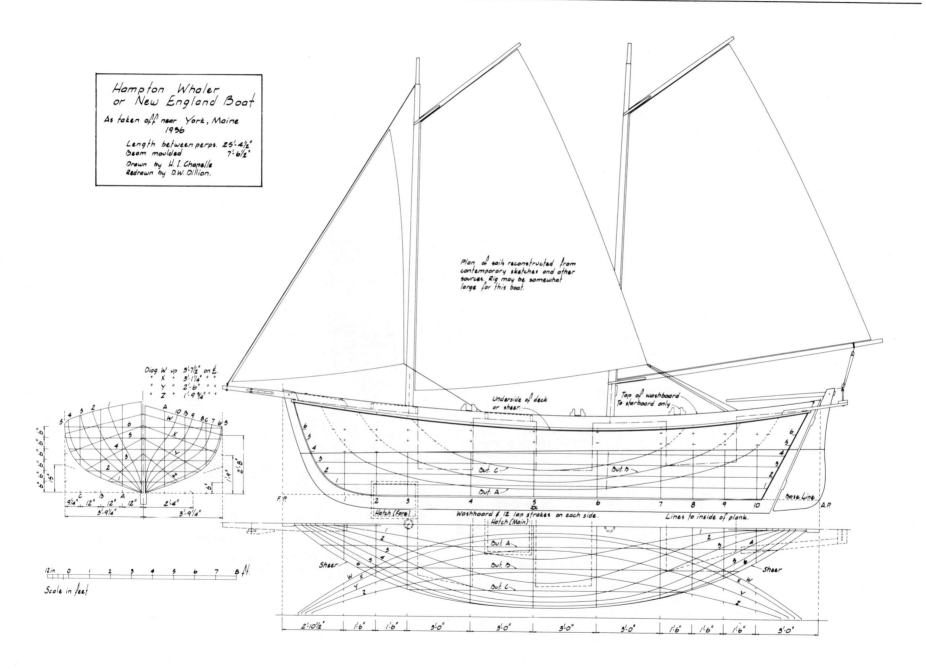

Hampton Whaler
or New England Boat

As taken off near York, Maine
1936

Length between perps. 25'-4½"
Beam moulded   7'-6½"

Drawn by H. I. Chapelle
Redrawn by D.W. Dillion.

Plan of sails reconstructed from contemporary sketches and other sources. Rig may be somewhat large for this boat.

Diag. W up 3'-7½" on €.
  "   X   " 3'-1¼" " "
  "   Y   " 2'-6"   " "
  "   Z   " 1'-9¾" " "

Underside of deck or sheer.

Top of washboard
To starboard only

Base Line

Hatch (Fore)

Washboard & 12 lap strakes on each side.

Hatch (Main)

Lines to inside of plank.

But. A
But. B
But. C

But. C
But. B
But. A

Sheer
Sheer

12in 0 1 2 3 4 5 6 7 8 ft.
Scale in feet

9¼" 12" 12" 12" 2'-4"
3'-9¼"   3'-9¼"

2'-8"
1'-9"

2'-10½" 1'-6" 1'-6" 3'-0" 3'-0" 3'-0" 3'-0" 1'-6" 1'-6" 1'-6" 3'-0"

Hampton whaler or New England boat.

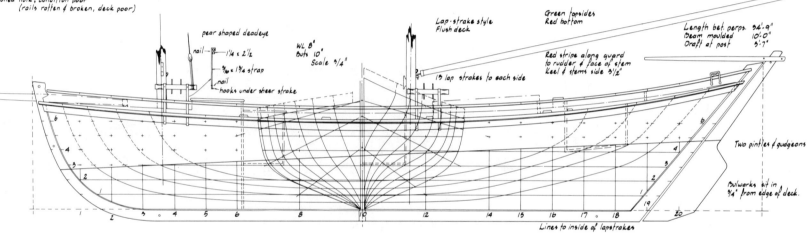

"English coast type"

Trial Drawing
Gaspe Boat as taken off
at St. Pierre Que.
No. 3

Original work by
Howard I. Chapelle
Redrawn for publication
by D.W. Dillion, Jun. 1984.

Boat about 21 years old according to nearby
resident (fisherman).
abandoned hulk, condition poor
(rails rotten & broken, deck poor)

Lap-strake style
Flush deck

Green topsides
Red bottom

pear shaped deadeye

nail — 1¼ x 2½

³⁄₁₆ x 1¾ strap

nail — hooks under sheer strake

WL 8"
Buts 10"
Scale ¾"

13 lap strakes to each side

Red stripe along guard
to rudder & face of stem
Keel & stems side 3½"

Length bet. perps. 34'-9"
Beam moulded 10'-0"
Draft at post 3'-7"

Two pintles & gudgeons

Bulwarks sit in
¾" from edge of deck.

Lines to inside of lapstrakes

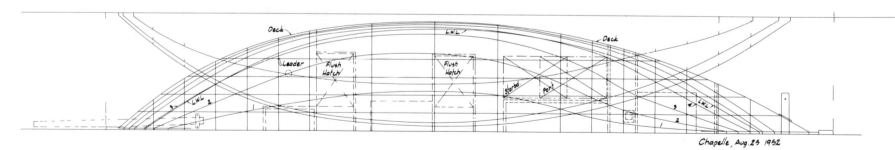

Deck
L.W.L.
Deck

Leader
Flush Hatch
Flush Hatch
Starbd
Port

L.W.L.
L.W.L.

Chapelle, Aug. 23 1952

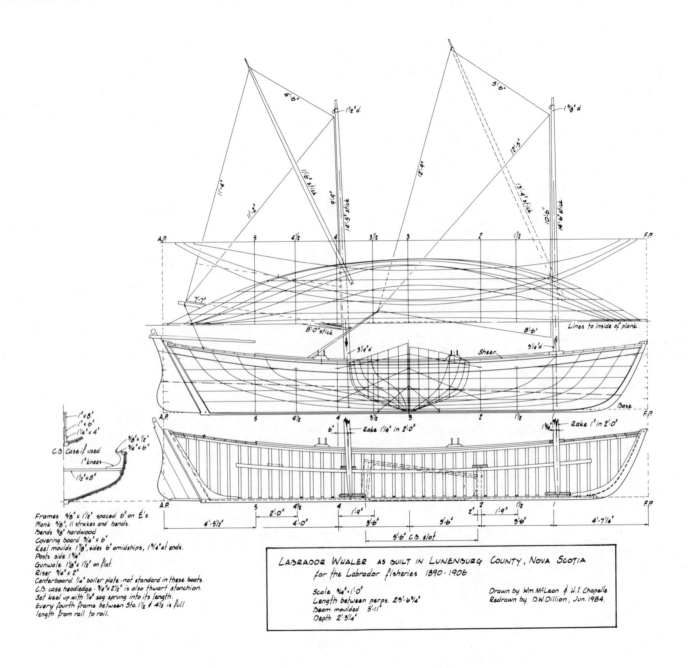

Frames 3/8" x 1 1/2" spaced 6" on E's.
Plank 5/8", 11 strakes and bends.
Bends 3/8" hardwood
Covering board 3/4" x 6"
Keel moulds 1 7/8", sides 6" amidships, 1 3/4" at ends.
Posts side 1 3/4"
Gunwale 1 1/8" x 1 1/2" on flat.
Riser 3/4" x 2"
Centerboard 1/4" boiler plate · not standard in these boats.
C.B. case headledge · 3/4" x 2 1/2" is also thwart stanchion.
Set keel up with 1/4" sag sprung into its length.
Every fourth frame between Sta. 1 1/2 & 4 1/2 is full
length from rail to rail.

LABRADOR WHALER AS BUILT IN LUNENBURG COUNTY, NOVA SCOTIA
for the Labrador fisheries 1890·1906

Scale 3/4" = 1'·0"   Drawn by Wm. McLean & H.I. Chapelle
Length between perps. 23'·6 3/4"   Redrawn by O.W. Dillion, Jun. 1984.
Beam moulded 5'·11"
Depth 2'·3 3/4"

Labrador whaler.

Elijah, a replica of a double-ended Hampton boat of the mid-19th century, is similar to the type mentioned in Audubon's account quoted on page 4.

sheer forward typical of the Tancook whalers. Certainly there are direct Hampton-Tancook resemblances, even with no transitional type. When David Stevens, surviving patriarch of a preeminent Tancook Island boat-building family, was shown a picture of the *Elijah*, a replica of an 1848 (Maine) Hampton boat, he commented, "You've got a whaler there. All you have to do is enlarge her, make the stem a little higher, and add a little more rake to the stern."

Be that as it may, the "All you have to do . . ." amounts to quite a bit, and the *Elijah* is considerably different from the Tancook whaler in its final form, as exemplified by the Middle River boat. Actually, by the end of the 19th century at least ten distinct types of double-ended workboats had emerged along the North Atlantic coast, ranging upward

from the Peapod, a fifteen-to-twenty footer developed in the 1870s for the Maine lobster fishery. Like the Peapod, each came from a specific locale and often was dubbed with a colorful local name such as Block Island Cowhorn, though some models were eventually adapted more widely.

Perhaps most important was the range of types that went under the name pinky. Following the invention of the mackerel jig around 1815, the double-ended pinky schooner gained in popularity as the Grand Banks fishery developed. Because fish move largely to the windward on the surface, a Grand Banks vessel had to be weatherly; with their deep draft and easy lines, pinky schooners filled the bill admirably. Built stoutly, they were as a rule of double-sawn frame construction with

Gaspe Bay pinky.

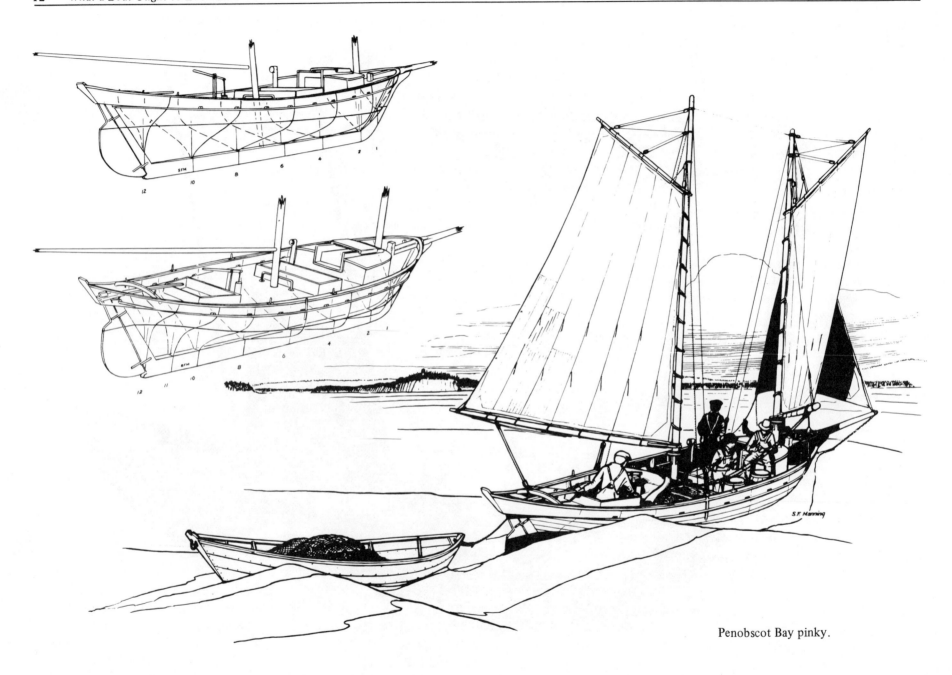

Penobscot Bay pinky.

A Crotch Island pinky as reproduced
by the Apprenticeshop in 1974-75.

lodging and hanging knees at every deck beam. By the 1820s a boat had
developed that was full-ended with straight rising floors, and this was
the design adopted by Maine builders in the following two decades.

One well-known type of Maine pinky was the Crotch Islander, a fast
and powerful design that Chapelle dates to 1880. It was built on the
Casco Bay mainland at such places as Yarmouth and Freeport as well as
on Crotch (now Cliff) Island. There was also the Eastport pinky, a late
form that Chapelle calls the "most developed type." Ordinarily these
did not go too far offshore, so the hull type could be more extreme
(Chapelle describes an 1855 half-model's lines as "very like those of the
extreme Baltimore clipper schooners of the slave trade type, the only
difference being the stern"). Eastport pinkys did, however, venture up
the coast; customhouse records in Halifax show vessels from Eastport
and Lubec frequently in port in late summer. The Canadians would no
doubt have admired such a good-looking and sharp-sailing boat, and
there are some striking similarities to the Tancook designs.

* * *

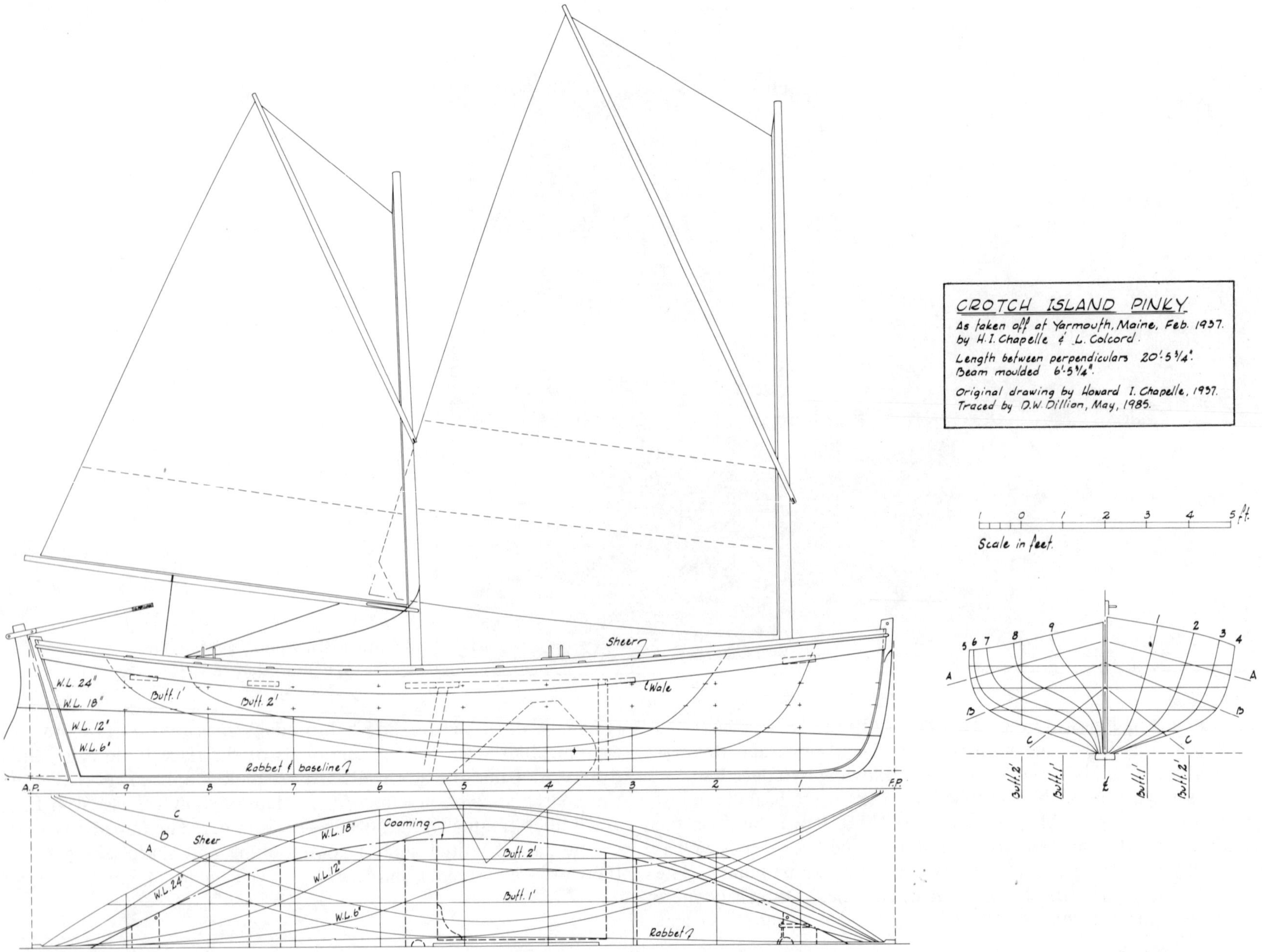

CROTCH ISLAND PINKY.
As taken off at Yarmouth, Maine, Feb. 1937.
by H.I.Chapelle & L.Colcord.
Length between perpendiculars 20'-5¾".
Beam moulded 6'-5¼".

Original drawing by Howard I. Chapelle, 1937.
Traced by D.W.Dillion, May, 1985.

Scale in feet.

Sheer

Wale

W.L. 24"
W.L. 18"
W.L. 12"
W.L. 6"
Butt. 1'
Butt. 2'

Rabbet & baseline

A.P.   9   8   7   6   5   4   3   2   1   F.P.

c
A   b   Sheer   Coaming
W.L. 18"
W.L. 24"   W.L. 12"   Butt. 2'
W.L. 6'   Butt. 1'

Rabbet

A   A
B   B
C   C

Butt. 2'   Butt. 1'   Butt. 1'   Butt. 2'

5 6 7   8   9   1   2   3   4

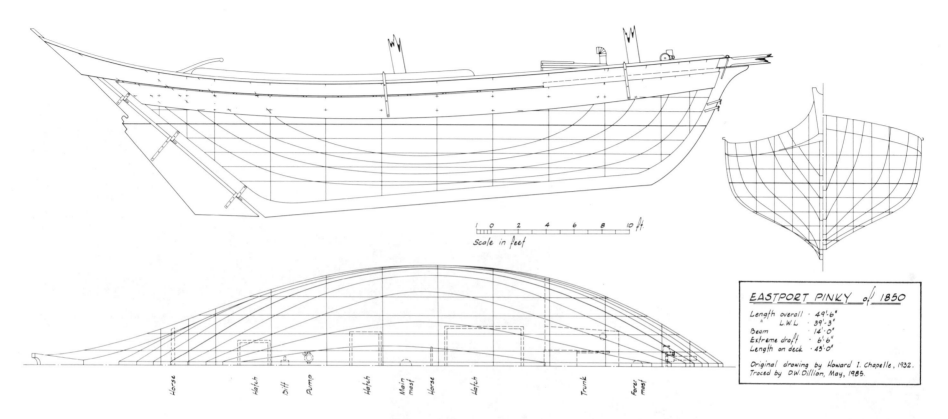

Scale in feet

EASTPORT PINKY of 1850

Length overall · 49'-6"
"   L.W.L · 39'-3"
Beam   · 14'-0"
Extreme draft · 6'-6"
Length on deck · 43'-0"

Original drawing by Howard I. Chapelle, 1932.
Traced by D.W.Dillion, May, 1985.

Horse   Hatch   Bitt   Pump   Hatch   Main mast   Horse   Hatch   Trunk   Fore mast

Maritime buffs will never tire of attempting to trace lines of design evolution. Yet, given the fragmentary state of the documentation, given a heritage of sharp-sterned workboats that extends back through centuries, and given certain concepts that undoubtedly were developed simultaneously rather than diffusing from a single point of origin (and were based partly on general assumptions about "what a boat ought to look like"), it may be debatable whether genealogical exercises on behalf of the Tancook whaler warrant any sustained effort.

The perils of attempting to trace lineage from one region to another are complicated by the considerable uncertainty about the Tancook whaler's *specific* origins. Tancook Islanders to whom Chapelle talked in the late 1940s indicated that the first Tancook whaler had actually been built on the mainland, at Lunenburg, between 1860 and 1870. Descendents of early Tancook builders who were interviewed in 1977 generally indicated, however, that the first whaler had been built on the island by Alfred Langille. But the ambiguity was often palpable. Langille's grandson Vernon declared, "I imagine he built the first one on Tancook." Interpretation of that statement turns entirely on the presence or absence of a pause after "the first one."

Whether or not anyone else built a Tancook whaler before Alfred Langille, he and his sons and grandsons—along with Amos Stevens and his descendents and two other boatbuilding families, the Masons and the Heislers—were responsible for most of the original whalers. And nobody disputes that the first whaler built on Tancook was the handiwork of Alfred Langille. The date remains an open question; some islanders thought it might have been as late as 1880, although Vernon Langille believed it was much earlier, in 1840 or 1850, which is conceivable inasmuch as his grandfather was born in 1821. If we split the difference and

Built at Lunenburg in 1916, the
Tancook whaler *Hazel R* measured
42'x11'2"x5'1". (MMA)

This photo of the *Hazel R* taken in
the 1930s by George Stadel shows
how she was altered for power by
adding a falsepiece on the sternpost
and cutting down the rudder.

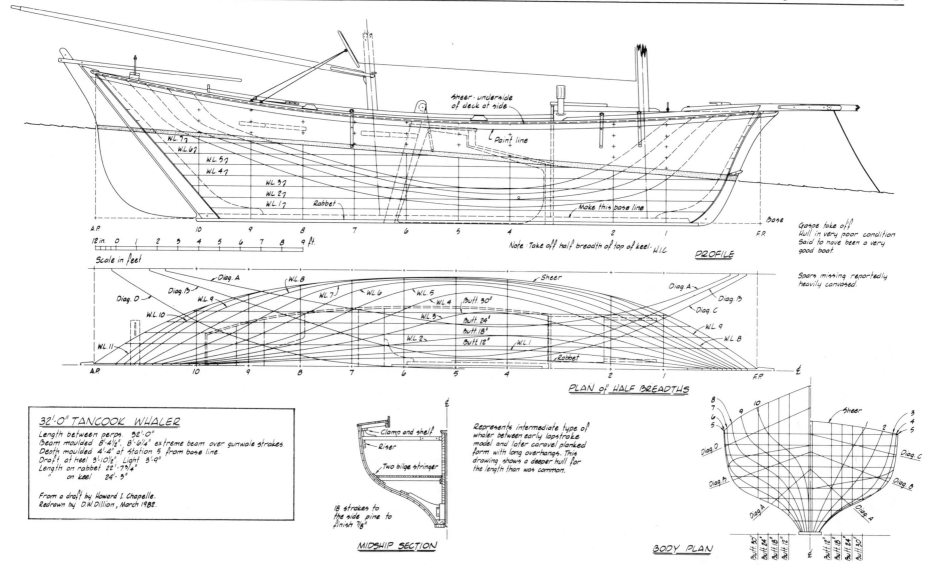

PROFILE

Scale in feet

12 in. 0 1 2 3 4 5 6 7 8 9 ft.

Note: Take off half breadth of top of keel. H.I.C.

Sheer: underside of deck at side

Paint line

Make this base line

Gaspe take off.
Hull in very poor condition
Said to have been a very
good boat.

PLAN of HALF BREADTHS

Spars missing reportedly
heavily canvased.

32'-0" TANCOOK WHALER

Length between perps. 32'-0"
Beam moulded 8'-4½", 8'-6¼" extreme beam over gunwale strakes.
Depth moulded 4'-4" at Station 5 from base line.
Draft at heel 3'-10½". Light 3'-9"
Length on rabbet 22'-7¾"
   "   on keel 24'-3"

From a draft by Howard I. Chapelle.
Redrawn by D.W. Dillion, March 1982.

MIDSHIP SECTION

Clamp and shelf
Riser
Two bilge stringer

18 strakes to
the side pine to
finish ⅞"

Represents intermediate type of
whaler between early lapstrake
model and later caravel planked
form with long overhangs. This
drawing shows a deeper hull for
the length than was common.

BODY PLAN

date the first whalers from 1860, we have a type of vessel that was built over a period of fifty years or a little more. Certainly they changed in that half century—later ones were commonly forty-five feet or even fifty, and lapstrake construction had given way to what the islanders called "seamwork"–and yet the basic design, as with all classics, seemed immutable. The "lines-man" *nonpareil* was Howard Chapelle, so let him tell something of the way they were:

"They had very raking sternposts and bald clipper bows in which the rabbets followed the stem profile. They were fitted with boiler-plate centerboards and drew about 4 feet with the board up; stone ballast

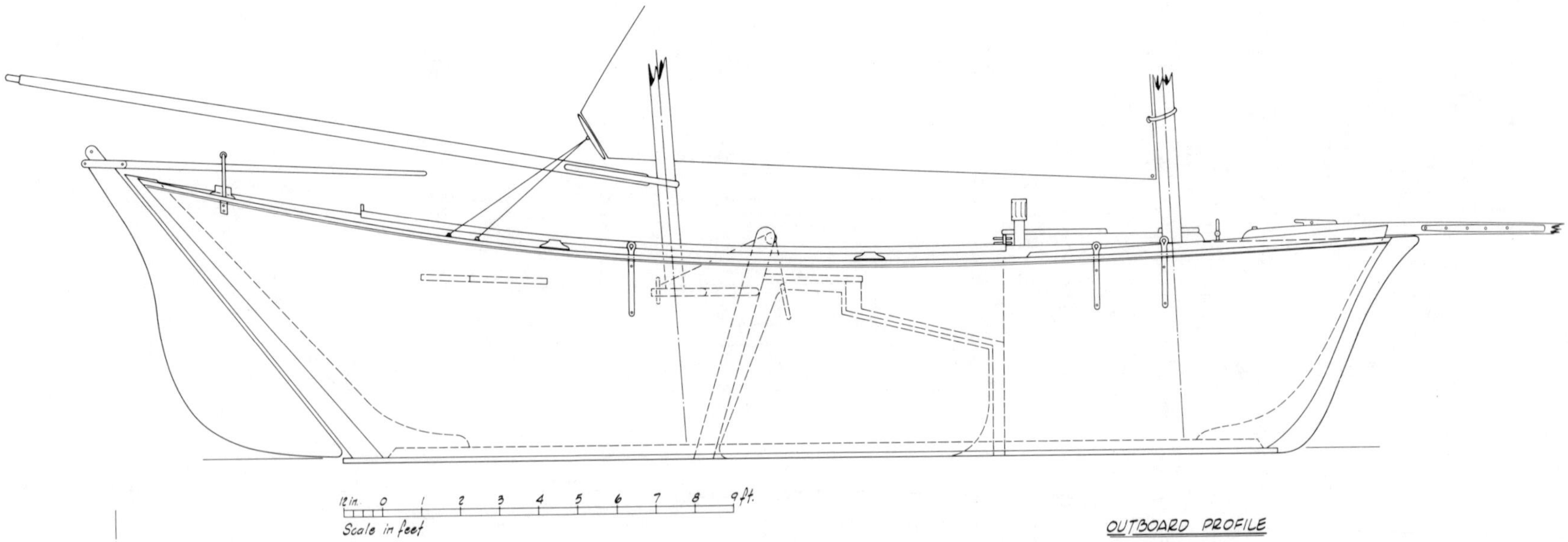

OUTBOARD PROFILE

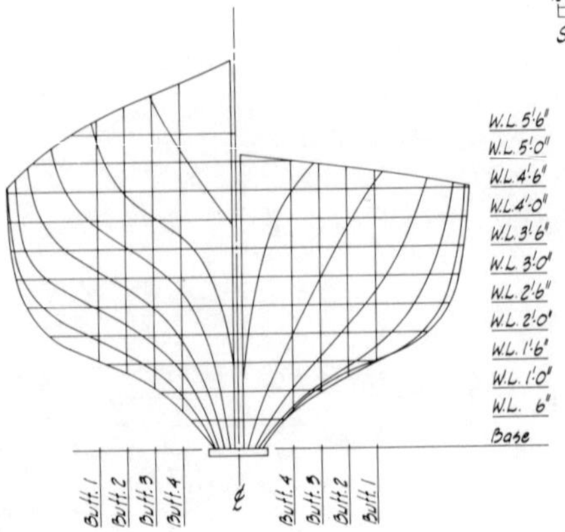

12 in. 0   1   2   3   4   5   6   7   8   9 ft.
Scale in feet

W.L 5'6"
W.L. 5'.0"
W.L. 4'.6"
W.L 4'.0"
W.L 3'.6"
W.L 3'.0"
W.L. 2'.6"
W.L. 2'.0"
W.L. 1'.6"
W.L. 1'.0"
W.L. 6"
Base

Butt.1 Butt.2 Butt.3 Butt.4   Butt.4 Butt.3 Butt.2 Butt.1

BODY PLAN

32'-0" TANCOOK WHALER

Length between perpendiculars · 32'.0"
Beam moulded · 8'.4½"
Beam extreme over gunwale · 8'.6¼"
Depth moulded (at Sta.5 from base) · 4'.4"
Load draft at heel · 3'.10½"
Light draft at heel · 3'.8"
Length on rabbet · 22'.7¾"
Length on keel · 24'.3"

Lines to inside of plank.
18 strakes per side, ⅞" thick, carvel built.

This boat represents an intermediate type of whaler between early lapstrake models and the later carvel built vessels with long overhangs.
The drawing shows a hull deeper in proportion to length than was usual.

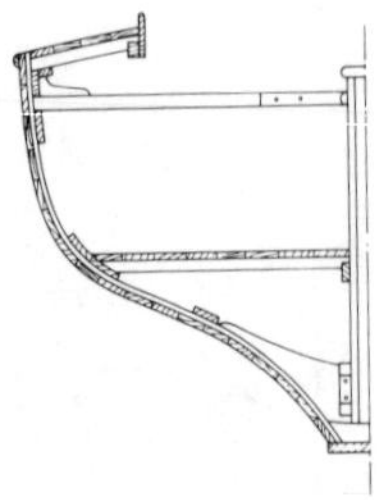

MIDSHIP SECTION

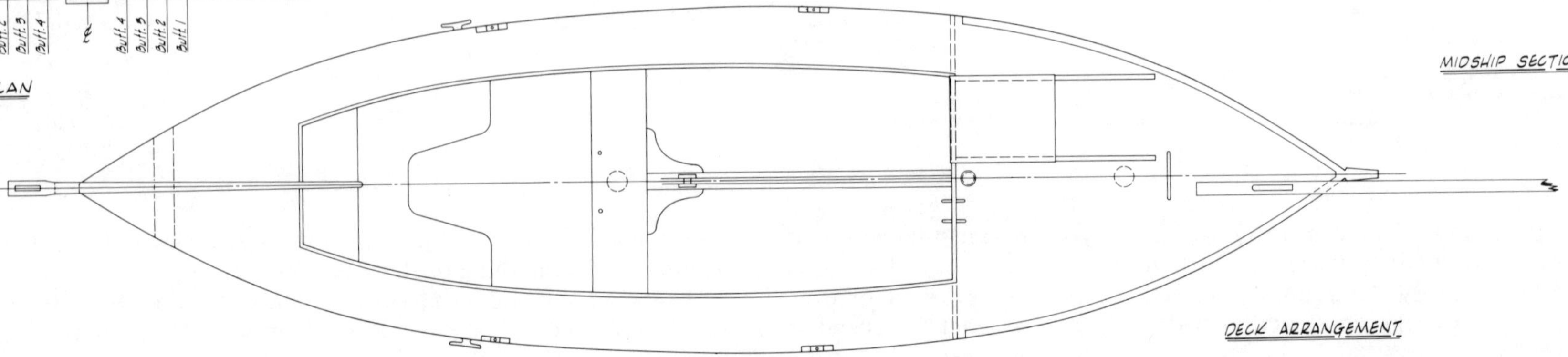

DECK ARRANGEMENT

Laying to a dock, this Tancook whaler shows off her fine lines. Courtesy of The Mariners Museum, Newport News, Virginia

was also carried. They usually had a flush deck forward, under which was a cabin with two platform berths and a stove. Abaft the cabin was a large oval cockpit. The side decks were quite narrow and the deck at the stern was quite short. The cockpit was divided by bulkheads or "parting boards" into standing rooms and fish holds; one of the parting boards was located at the main thwart, which served to support the mainmast. A low finger rail ran around the deck at the sheer; in some of the boats this rail was substantial and was extended abaft the rudderhead, as in the pinky stern. The ends of this projection were joined by a bolt passing through a length of pipe, which acted as a spacer to fix the ends of the projecting rail pieces at the proper distance apart. The pipe served as a main-sheet horse. This may have been an adaptation of the New Hampshire boat's stern outrigger under the influence of the pinky; the latter was a very well-known type in Nova Scotia.

"The lines of the Tancook whalers were remarkably sharp; the midsection showed a very hollow garboard and hard bilge; the wide plank keel was another feature. The boats sat low in the water and had a very graceful sheer. Altogether the Tancook whaler was one of the most handsome of the double-enders used on the Atlantic Coast. . . ."

* * *

Any sailor who ponders photos of Tancook's whalers assumes that they were tender. The beam-to-length ratio was close to one to four, the beam a bit more than twice the draft at the post—"It would probably be very difficult to make the hull finer without losing power to carry sail," Chapelle observed—and so the low schooner rig with a big, club-headed main topmast staysail was well suited to the form of the hull. Local conditions off the Atlantic coast of Tancook imposed a rigorous set of related design requirements. The Islanders often fished thirty miles away, sometimes even further. In summer morning calms they often had to row for miles and miles, and often they had to run home fast ahead of a rising gale. Vernon Langille, who allowed as how he had been a "keen sailor," stated that in a nor'wester he could beat up to the island in a whaler while others scudded off.

Chapelle was intrigued with the construction of the Middle River boat. When he found the boat it had been beached for some twenty years, after having been in service for about fifteen. Made entirely of local species of timber, "many of which are held in dispute in yacht

building," it still had withstood the elements well enough to enable the making of an accurate set of lines. "There were not above seven bolts in the entire hull structure," Chapelle observed, "excepting the small ones used to secure the ironwork. Spikes had been used in the floor timbers and part of the deadwood; the remaining fastenings were boat nails." Posts were formed from the lower trunk and roots of larch trees, the outer shoe was elm or beech, the keel appeared to be birch, and there was no rabbet. Chapelle thought it notable that the floor knees were not connected with the light frames; rather, they were "tied together only by their common fastening to the keel and lower hull planking." The floors were spruce knees, the planking "a local 'pine,' which was harder than any white pine I have seen, and seemed to be an eastern fir with which I am unacquainted." The one aspect of the design of which he disapproved was the centerboard, which was shaped so that little of it would remain in the case when lowered, thereby straining its supporting trunk structure.

As to the more cosmetic aspects of the Tancook whaler, Bell had noted that the sails "were nearly always tanned," while a reminiscence by Edwin Pugsley describes a whaler with its light staysail soaked in a solution of hemlock bark which dyed it almost black: "In a rain or fog the drippings would blacken anything they touched." There are photos showing whalers with all sails black. While Ernest Bell had referred to a white-hulled whaler, and Chapelle had heard of a gray one, Pugsley had been told that they "were commonly black, a number were dark bottle green, and most of those had black sheer strakes." Bottoms were red, decks gray.

According to Bell, a forty-six-foot whaler built around 1913, complete and ready to go fishing with sails and two dories, cost $450. In 1894 Amos Stevens had sold a whaler to the Royal Engineers, Halifax—slated to join the Nova Scotia Yacht Squadron—for $300. These prices sound nominal, and yet one must remember that the whaler was an easily built boat—"much simpler than a schooner," as David Stevens observed. Vernon Langille said that the time involved in construction was two or three months. "They just ran a straight stem up and a straight stern," explained David Stevens. "For a schooner you have to get around the tuck, and that makes it harder to plank. I found there was just nothing to it, planking up a Tancook whaler."

Ease of construction may well have been an important consideration for David's grandfather when he started building whalers. Amos Stevens

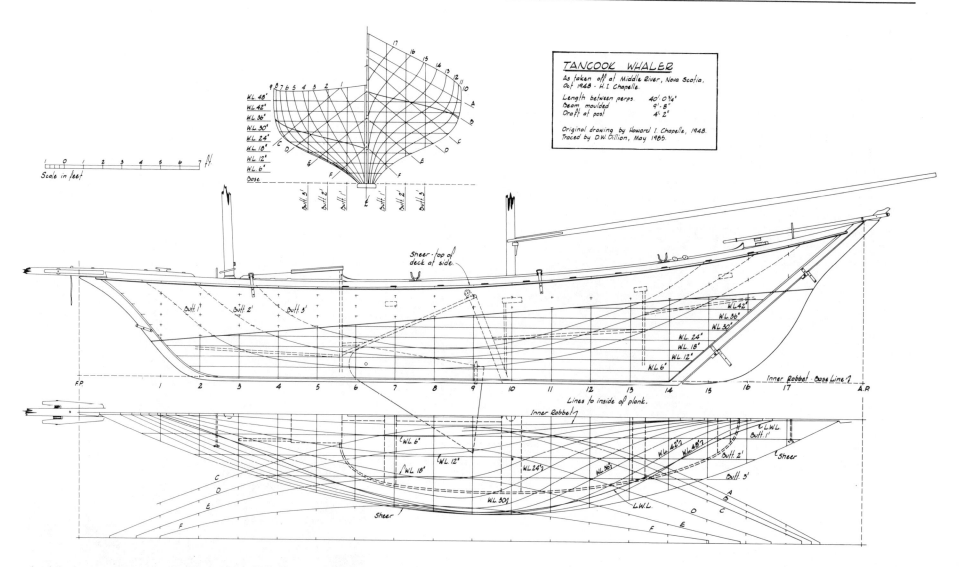

had been a teamster in Halifax before he moved his large family to Tancook Island to make his living by farming and fishing. As a boatbuilder he was a fast learner, soon an innovator. He became known as the master builder of Tancook, the first to switch from lapstrake construction to seamwork, around the turn of the century. Vernon Langille,

who built his first boat in 1901, stated that aside from punts and dories, "I never built any lapstrake boats." Amos Stevens was also the first Tancook builder to experiment with transom sterns and spoon bows, seen on the larger schooners sailing out of Lunenburg. Ultimately he developed a distinctive new type, more burdensome than the whaler,

A lapstraked Tancook whaler with tanbark sails drifts out of Halifax harbor. (MMA)

Stern view of a Tancook whaler showing planking detail. (MMA)

A Tancook schooner, a later whaler variation with transom and engine. Photograph taken by George Stadel in Lunenburg County in the 1930s.

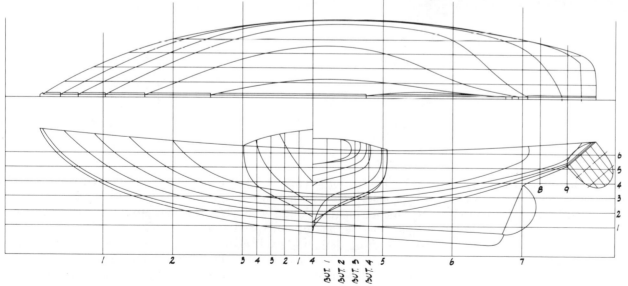

From John McLean & Sons, Ltd.
Mahone Bay
for a pleasure boat on Tancook
fishing schooner · boat model · 1925.
L.O.A.   40'. 0"
L.W.L.   30'. 9"
Depth (moulded) Sec. 4   5'. 3"
Beam (moulded)   10'. 3"
Originally drawn at scale: 1/2":1'
Redrawn to 3/8":1'-0"
by D.W. Dillion, April, 1984.

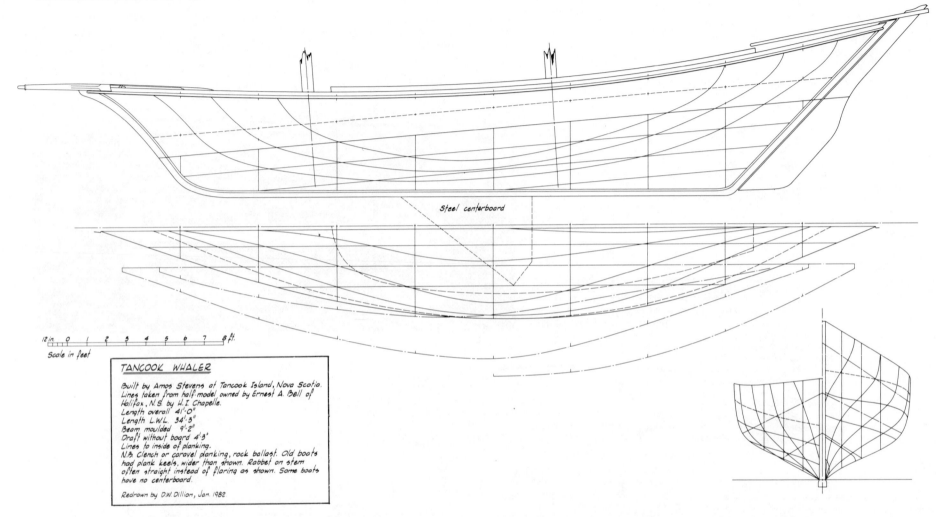

Scale in feet

TANCOOK WHALER

Built by Amos Stevens at Tancook Island, Nova Scotia.
Lines taken from half-model owned by Ernest A. Bell of
Halifax, N.S. by H.I. Chapelle.
Length overall 41'-0"
Length L.W.L. 34'-3"
Beam moulded 9'-2"
Draft without board 4'-3"
Lines to inside of planking.
N.B. Clench or caravel planking, rock ballast. Old boats
had plank keels, wider than shown. Rabbet on stem
often straight instead of flaring as shown. Some boats
have no centerboard.

Redrawn by D.W. Dillion, Jan. 1982

the Tancook schooner. And that marked the beginning of the end for the whaler as a workboat; another member of the Stevens clan who was born in 1922 said that by the twenties "the whaler was gone. Grandfather was building schooners."

* * *

Well, no, the whaler was not gone entirely, for, even while the last workboats were disappearing, the design was attracting the eye of yachtsmen in the U.S. as well as Canada. Because of the whaler's handsome lines, good turn of speed, and seakeeping qualities, all honed to the exacting demands of Tancook's inshore fisheries, certain of Tancook's most venerable boatbuilding families—the Stevenses in particular—continued to build them on the mainland as pleasure boats. And

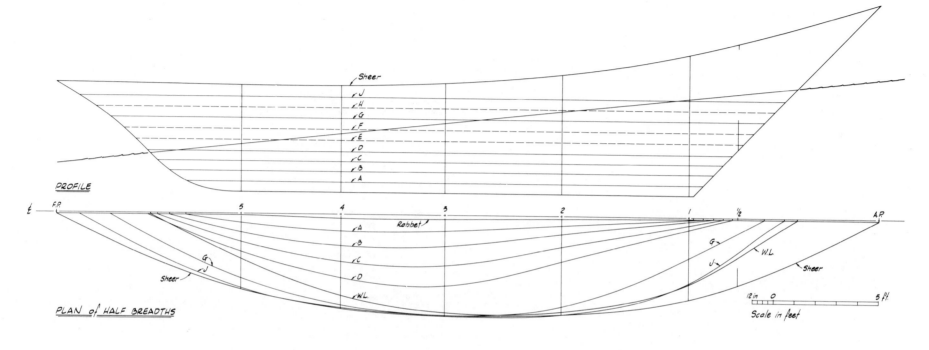

Sheer
J
H
G
F
E
D
C
B
A

PROFILE

F.P.   5   4   3   2   1   ½   A.P.

A
Rabbet
B
G
C
U
D
W.L.

Sheer
G
J

Sheer

W.L.

12 in   0   5 ft.

Scale in feet

PLAN of HALF BREADTHS

THE "La Have" MODEL
39'-8" between perpendiculars, 9'-5" beam, 4'-6" draft.
Lines from the model to inside of plank.
Taken by D.W.Dillion, May 1982.   Scale ¾": 1'-0"
Model from Refuse Shipyard, La Have River, Bridgewater, N.S.
Model owned by Mr. Nathanial West, Vineyard Haven, Mass.
Station ½ added to gain shape of W.L. & level line "J".
Lines developed by scaling offsets from separated lifts.
Dotted lifts not separated.

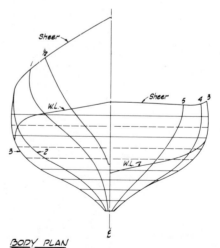

Sheer
½
1
Sheer
5 4 3
W.L.
3 2
W.L.

BODY PLAN

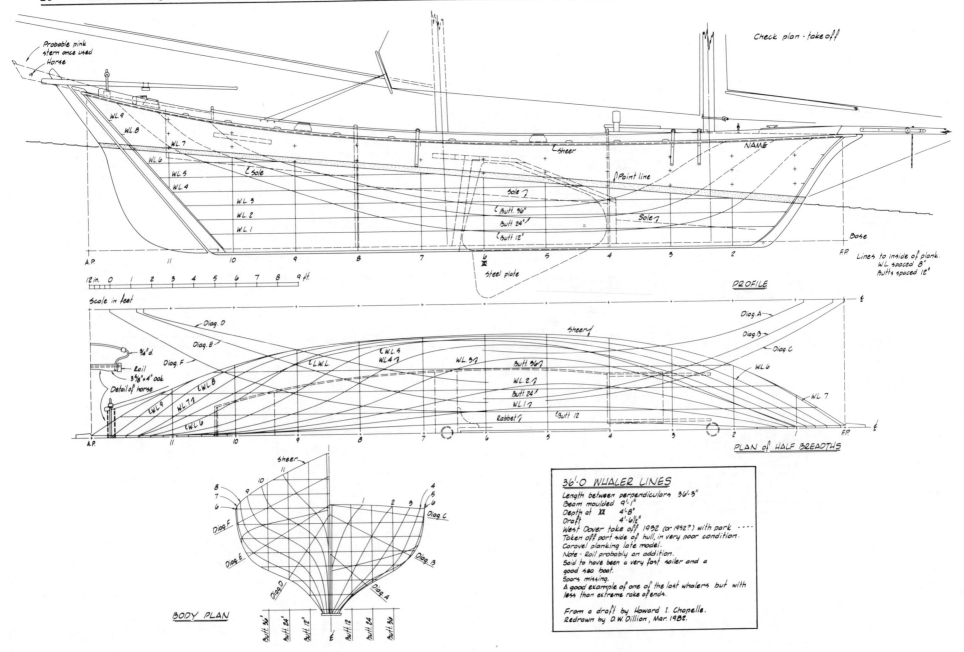

Check plan · take off

Probable pink stern once used Horse

WL.9
WL.8
WL.7
WL.6
WL.5
WL.4
WL.3
WL.2
WL.1

Sole

Sheer

Name

Point line

Sole

Butt. 36"
Butt 24"
Sole
Butt 12"

Base

A.P.   11   10   9   8   7   6   5   4   3   2   F.P.

steel plate

Lines to inside of plank.
WL spaced 8"
Butts spaced 12"

PROFILE

12 in. 0 1 2 3 4 5 6 7 8 9 ft.
Scale in feet

Diag. D
Diag. E
Diag. F

¾" d.
Rail
3⅝"×4" oak
Detail of horse

LWL.8
LWL 9
WL.7
LWL 6

Sheer

LWL
WL.5
WL.4

WL.3

Butt. 36

WL.2
Butt. 24
WL.1
Rabbet   Butt 12

Diag. A
Diag. B
Diag. C

WL.6

WL.7

A.P.   11   10   9   8   7   6   5   4   3   2   1   F.P.

PLAN of HALF BREADTHS

sheer
10 11
8 9
7
6
4
5
6
2 3

Diag. F
Diag. E
Diag. D
Diag. C
Diag. B
Diag. A

Butt 36" Butt 24" Butt 12"   Butt 12 Butt 24 Butt 36

BODY PLAN

36'·0 WHALER LINES

Length between perpendiculars 36'·3"
Beam moulded 9'·1"
Depth at XI 4'·8"
Draft 4'·6½"
West Dover take off 1932 (or 1952?) with park · · · ·
Token off port side of hull, in very poor condition.
Carvel planking late model.
Note · Rail probably an addition.
Said to have been a very fast sailer and a
good sea boat.
Spars missing.
A good example of one of the last whalers but with
less than extreme rake of ends.

From a draft by Howard I. Chapelle.
Redrawn by D.W. Dillion, Mar. 1982.

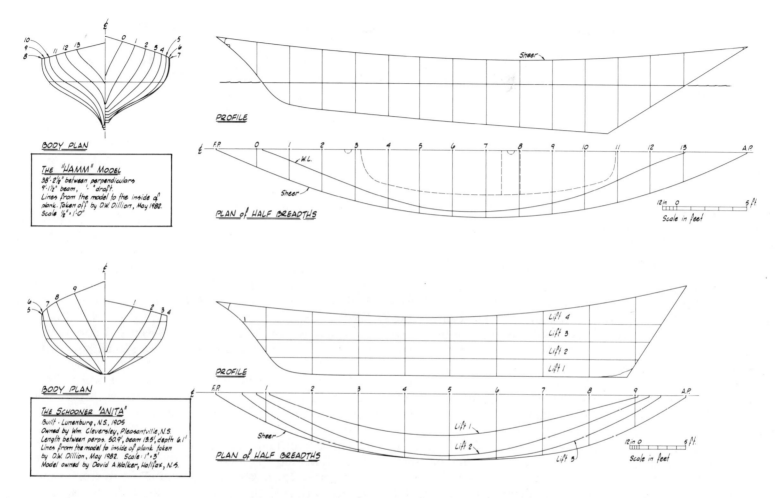

BODY PLAN

THE "HAMM" MODEL
38'·2⅛" between perpendiculars
9'·1½" beam, '·" draft.
Lines from the model to the inside of
plank. Taken off by D.W. Dillion, May 1982.
Scale ⅛" : 1'-0"

PROFILE

PLAN of HALF BREADTHS

Scale in feet

BODY PLAN

THE SCHOONER "ANITA"
Built · Lunenburg, N.S., 1905
Owned by Wm. Cleversley, Pleasantville, N.S.
Length between perps. 50.9', beam 13.5', depth 6.1'
Lines from the model to inside of plank taken
by D.W. Dillion, May 1982. Scale: 1" : 3'
Model owned by David A.Walker, Halifax, N.S.

PROFILE

Lift 4
Lift 3
Lift 2
Lift 1

Lift 1
Lift 2
Lift 3

PLAN of HALF BREADTHS

Scale in feet

more recently, builders in New England, on Chesapeake Bay, and even on the West Coast, have been producing whalers as yachts.

To be sure, in the eye of a purist, even the most carefully crafted of these pleasure boats cannot match the virtues of the original workboats; at very least the low freeboard with swooping sheer, which permitted rowing with sweeps, will have been modified. Even the *Vernon Langille*, built from Chapelle's lines using traditional methods, admittedly has "some modern touches." Still, the *Langille* more closely resembles the

Tancook Island workboats than anything else built in sixty years or more, and its visit to the island in 1979 was a memorable event. Tancook Island is not the place it once was; there are only a third as many residents as in 1911, and no boatbuilders. The *Langille*, then, was reminiscent of Tancook in its heyday, just before a series of economic and technological changes drastically modified its social patterns. Next, we take a look at some of these patterns and at some history on Tancook Island.

2 A Place Called Tancook

As with many similar places, more than one plausible explanation exists for the origins of the name *Tancook*. The Micmac name for the Tancooks (there is a Little Tancook as well as Great Tancook) was *uktancook*, meaning "facing the open sea." Yet the name inevitably has a folk-etymology too. L.B. Jenson, who knows local lore as well as anyone, writes, "I have heard from old fishermen that fishing nets were *tanned* and *cooked* there, i.e., boiled in water with bark in great iron pots." Whatever the true origin, by the end of the 18th century the name Tancook had superseded Queen Charlotte's Island (the name by which it once had been deeded to one Patrick Sutherland, Esq.) and was firmly established along the Atlantic coast of Nova Scotia.

Great Tancook stands at the entrance of Mahone Bay, five miles from Chester to the northwest and thirty from Halifax to the northeast. It is on about the same latitude as Bangor, Maine, but its eastern shore is almost fully exposed to the Atlantic (recall the Micmac "facing the open sea"). On December 19, 1792, it was granted to John Henry Fleiger and George Grant, along with Little Tancook and nearby Starr Island, "the whole of said islands being wilderness lands. . . ."

A memorandum dated June 11, 1788, and annexed to the original plan, tells us something of what Tancook was like as a wilderness:

"Great Tancook Island contains 550 acres of land. It is in general good hardwood land—beech, birch, and maple, and some oak, and ash. There are several small rivulets and springs, which afford good water. It has no harbor, and water is shoal on the Mahone Bay side, so that there is no anchorage within two hundred yards, even for small schooners.

"Upon a moderate calculation, there may be about ten thousand cords of wood, and some timber trees for building."

Though Tancook's natural attributes were mixed, it would not have been altogether unappealing to Europeans seeking a new home. The first settlers were Germans and Englishmen. The British government sent French Huguenots to replace the expelled Acadians, and a wave of United Empire Loyalists who fled north during and after the American Revolution also settled there. Numbers were very small. When Thomas Haliburton published his *Historical and Statistical Account of Nova Scotia*, the first history of that province (1829), he recorded thirty resident families. In 1845 there were seventy children attending the public school. Half a century later there were 120 children with a total population of 465.

The fishing industry reached its peak of prosperity around the turn of the 20th century, and this coincided with the only period in Tancook's history that could conceivably be called a boom. Population doubled between 1895 and 1911, peaking at around 900. While fishing remained profitable through the war years, costs were rising faster than prices. Then competition from the growing Grand Banks fleet began to push prices downward. Those who chose to remain and work the shore fishery, writes Kathy Kuusisto (who, under the sponsorship of the Explorations Program of the Canada Council, interviewed many islanders in the 1970s), "were those most able to find a way to cope and to make the necessary sacrifices for survival." Those who left the island in the 1920s included all the boatbuilders, most of whom reestablished themselves on the mainland in the vicinity of Lunenburg, Nova Scotia's primary fishing port. Today, Tancook Island numbers 300 residents.

* * *

Life on a place such as Tancook could never have been easy. David Stevens, who carries on the family boatbuilding tradition at Second Peninsula near Lunenburg, ponders the situation that existed just before his family left:

"Us youngsters had no idea what the old folks had to go through. Fish in those times were dirt cheap—three or four dollars for a whole barrel of salted herring. Dad used to tell me that they would have to get up at two in the morning and start for the fishing grounds. And they'd have to row until they got a little wind and then put up the sails.

"When we were growing up, he didn't want us to have to do that. So that's the reason he came over here and bought the farm."

Still, David Stevens could readily understand what it was that had been attractive about Tancook: "It was a place to settle. You couldn't be too choosy. They raised the best beef, became famous for sauerkraut, and it was really a good place to live. And fishing was right near, so they could fish and farm. And they could build boats."

The whaler played a key role in the island fishing-farming economy. Nearly every family had a boat. Many built their own in wintertime; David Stevens estimated that at one time as many as three-fourths of the men on Tancook could build a boat. A boat under construction was a matter of keen interest, and people would make it a point to visit a shop—often, actually, just a barn, replete with farm animals—to size one up. "Criticize the other fellow's boat and brag your own up, that used to be quite the thing on Tancook Island," David Stevens recalls. "Of course, there were fellows who would go from one shop to the other, and they'd criticize and talk and talk and talk. And then, of course, the first thing in the spring, when they were in the water and rigged, there was a race around the island."

The competitive spirit among Tancookers (both Great Tancook and Little Tancook) and their mainland neighbors was partly to account for the fine lines and good turn of speed of the whalers, quite apart from the utility of a fast, easily driven hull in getting to and from the fishing grounds. An old-timer from Chester named E.A. Fader, who once bought a sloop from Amos Stevens, recalled that there had been formal races as early as 1885. Competitors were invited from the mainland towns of Lunenburg and Mahone Bay and from the two Tancooks. Among the latter there were "great arguments . . . about which was the better boat, the Little Tancook sloop or the Big Tancook whaler."

On racing technique, Fader continued,

"When running before the wind, wing and wing, or as the Tancook fishermen called it, 'split it open,' they had a pole to which they attached a staysail and hoisted it to the topmast, making a squaresail out of it which they called 'scandalizing the staysail.' Anyway it was very effective. I can still recall some of the old time greats that were renowned for their ability to handle a boat in any kind of weather. Big Tancooker David Baker was, I believe, the daddy of them all, closely followed by Al Langille, Hip Baker, Zip Wilson, Wesley and Leander Young. . . ."

Ernest Bell's engineer, recall, had identified the "Baker boys" as the ones "passing" in the Tancook whaler, and we will soon get better acquainted with the man Fader listed between David and Hip, Alfred Langille. Some men excelled as sailors, some as builders, some as both. And Alfred Langille was one of the latter. He was the first on Tancook to begin building boats for his neighbors and for residents of the mainland, that is, to become a commercial boatbuilder. His shop at Langille's Cove (part of South East Cove on the Atlantic shore of Big Tancook) became something of a local attraction. "I've never seen a man that could use a chisel as well as he could," says Perry Stevens, recalling boyhood visits to Al Langille's shop.

Langille was devoted to his craft, as is exemplified in this story:

"Give up boatbuilding," pleaded Mrs. Langille. "I just read in the paper that Halley's Comet is going to destroy the world. The world is coming to an end, so come up and sit down and rest until it happens."

"God Almighty, woman," he answered. "I want to get these garboards on the boat before it happens."

Such apocryphal tales always have an underlying reality, and in the case of a man like Langille the reality was that youngsters wanted to be like him, to do what he could do, as well as he could.

"When I was thirteen," recalled Langille's grandson Vernon, "I was going to school and my grandfather . . . used to fish in the summer and farm, and in the winter he built boats. So I asked him one day if I could have his boatshop and tools to build a boat, and he said yes.

"So on Saturdays when there was no school, I used to come up to Mahone Bay, and I bought all the lumber and got the nails and made the molds and got it all ready to start when school closed. The first one I built was around 20 or 21 feet overall. It had only three molds outside the sternpost mold and stem mold. . . .

"I knew what boat I wanted. I swept the shop floor off and took some battens, and I made the length I thought the bottom should be. Then I drew a line up through the stern plank, and I took a thin oak batten and lined the shape of the stem. Then I drew a centerline from stem to stern and marked the broadside out, the width that I thought the boat should be. Then I divided the sections up where I wanted the molds. And I took a little half-inch by quarter batten, and I bent the shape down to the bottom, where the bottom was supposed to be. And that's where I got the shape for the molds. And I built the boat."

This was how one thirteen-year-old started out as a boatbuilder. The story was repeated over and over, though not everybody remembers having had an easy time of it. David Stevens recalls the way it was at the shop of *his* grandfather, Amos Stevens, across the island:

"I remember when I was only a little rascal down at my grandfather's boatshop, when he was building actively, and I just couldn't keep away from his spokeshave. I'd get a piece of wood and get in there. He'd growl at me and tell me I was dulling his tools. I'd drop the tool, and out of the corner of my eye I'd see him go around to the other side of the boat, and I'd pick it up again. He didn't bother me too much.

"When I grew up I remembered this, and I thought if I ever have a son I'll certainly not growl at him. I'll put things in his way and make it easy for him to pick up a tool."

When a contingent from the Maine Maritime Museum visited David Stevens's shop in 1978, he was retired, having turned over the business to his son Murray. The elder Stevens was, however, busily building a forty-foot schooner from a half-model carved by his grandfather. His grandsons were helping him. So it is that in the Mahone Bay area, Tancook boatbuilding traditions pass from generation to generation.

* * *

So, too, it was with fishing, a pursuit that had to be established on a commercial basis to enable commercial boatbuilding. There is some question as to when fishing became the primary occupation on Tancook, though it was in the 1830s at the very earliest, for Haliburton had noted in 1829 that the islanders "derive their substance wholly from tilling the land." And, no matter when Tancookers took to the sea, fishing was always a seasonal occupation. Whalers, like other early fishing craft, were hauled on the beach in the winter and stored.

South East Cove of Big Tancook Island in 1905 showing six large Tancook whalers hauled on their individual ways. (MMA)

On good days in March they were painted, and by April they were generally back in the water, moored in either of two coves, South East or North West. Many fishermen kept a mooring in each cove, moving from one to the other to get a good lee when a storm threatened. Both were exposed to winds however, and a dependable mooring was essential. Mooring blocks were the heaviest stones that could be carried off the beach on timber supported across two dories. Every whaler was permanently fitted with an iron ring around the foremast, to which the mooring chain was hooked. Fastened to the chain itself was a wooden pole, as long as forty-five feet at the deeper and rougher South East Cove, where, as Tom Mason put it, "the sea would bellow right into the land." Perry Stevens observed that this mooring system "was better

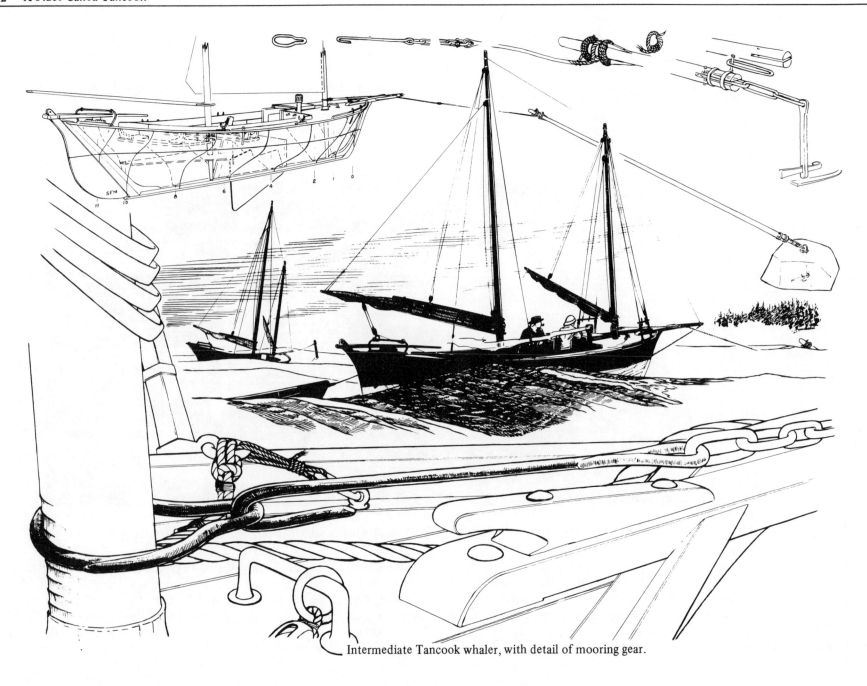

Intermediate Tancook whaler, with detail of mooring gear.

than an anchor because, if it blowed real hard, it would put that whole pole under water and then it would give. There would be no shock to it. It would be like having a spring."

When the boats were put back in the water, it was not yet time to go fishing. Rather, it was time to turn to the land and plant. The chief commercial crop was cabbage, which the Tancookers made into sauerkraut for sale in Halifax and elsewhere on the mainland. "Planting was a slow process," Perry Stevens observed, "because they had these ox teams to work with. That would be an interesting thing, too. They had yokes and they were very slow and the island is three miles long and a half-mile wide. One family in particular had property on the extreme northeast end and they also had property on the southwest end. When he went to make his hay with this pair of oxen . . . he could make one trip to get over around dinner hour and then by the time he got back it was supper time. Now they have trucks." Tancook Islanders also raised potatoes, mostly for home consumption, and a variety of herbs and vegetables. There was a rather strict division of labor with regard to planting; men planted the cabbage and potatoes, women the rest.

As for fishing, that was strictly men's work, although women played a big role when the catch was brought in. Fishermen went out two or three to a boat, father and son, or brothers—a boy learned from his father or from an uncle. Fishing for mackerel or herring was a matter of setting gill nets, about a quarter-mile's worth with a lantern-lit buoy at one end. The nets drifted with the boat all night, and a good catch would be sufficient to fill the boat completely.

Going after cod, haddock, and halibut was a matter of handlining, a technique Tom Mason describes so:

"In the old whalers, they had what they called the standing space where they steered. And that's where the skipper would fish from. He'd have a handline on each side. And then there'd be a thwart across and a bulkhead, and then there'd be a bin for fish from there to the mainmast. Then ahead of the mainmast there would be another section and that would be floored off as a passageway athwarts the ship where a man would be fishing. It was arranged so he could walk from one side to the other to tend his lines. And then beyond that would be another big bin for stowage or fishing gear, probably nets, too. Then in the old whalers, I think there used to be a narrow walkway forward right by the forecastle where a third man could fish back and forth, from side to side. . . .

"The handlines would be about 50 fathoms. What they would do is double, because the water would be deeper than 50 fathoms. And sometimes, if they didn't get to the depth of the water—they never fished in depth that would exceed a line and a half—they'd take a line and just cut it in the middle. In other words, they'd take three lines to make two.

"From the handline, which was hempline, you only used two hooks. . . . You had a lead sinker on the end, fastened to the line, and then from the other end of the sinker you'd have what we call the snoods going off with your hooks on. They'd be pretty near a fathom long, four or five feet long. When you'd haul up your fish, you'd first get your lead and you'd drop that on the boat and then you'd haul in the lines, and you might have two fish. . . .

"If you were drifting, then you'd just fish from the one side so the boat wouldn't drift over your lines. The only time you'd use both lines was if you struck a spot of fish, and then you'd anchor so you could fish from both sides."

Sometimes the Tancook fishermen started out at two or three in the morning, rowing with long spruce oars (twelve or even fourteen feet in length) until they caught a morning breeze. They would often stay out overnight, or even two or three nights, cooking meals on a fire built on the ballast. If they waited to leave the island until after dinner, their main meal at midday, they would have to beat out against the prevailing southwesterly breezes. Though Tancook whalers were not uncommon in fishing grounds off Halifax and Port Medway, ordinarily they fished directly out, on a series of underwater ridges running parallel to the coastline, from seven or eight to about thirty miles away.

Perry Stevens recalls the old days of fishing from Tancook:

"Off our shore the furthest island out is Pearl Island, and then the next place you'd come to was the first ridge. You'd go probably four or five miles farther and you'd come to the second ridge. The water shoaled up. We'd call it a hill on the land, or a mountain. Farther out was another place, a smaller place, called the Hummock. Then the farthest place they would go would be Doug's Ridge. That would be a better place to catch halibut.

"But the most fishing they done, they had nets, mackerel nets or herring nets. The water was too deep to anchor, so they set them all out in front and had a long rope tied up to the nets. They called that droguing.

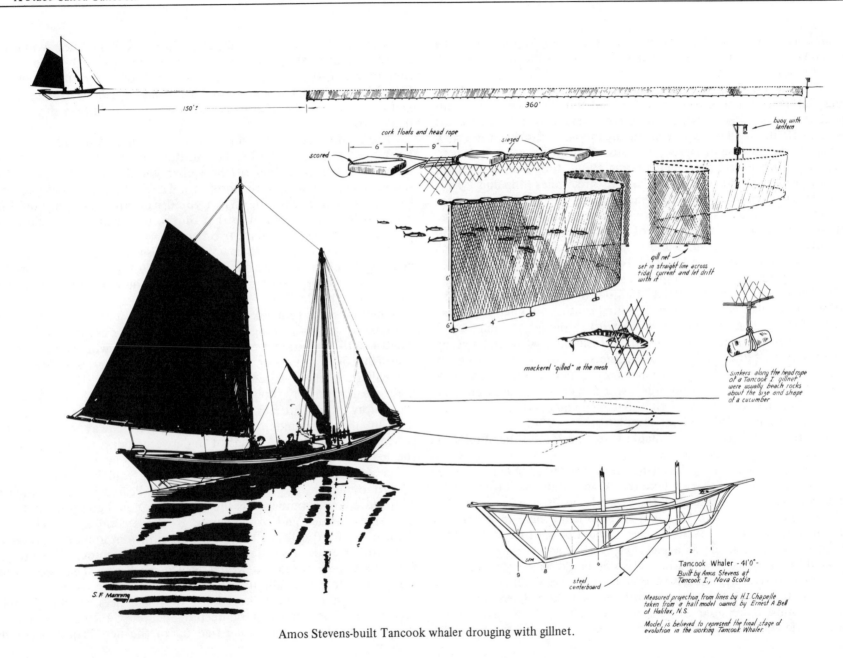

cork floats and head rope

scored

siezed

buoy with lantern

gill net set in straight line across tidal current and let drift with it

6'

6'   4'

mackerel "gilled" in the mesh

sinkers along the head rope of a Tancook I gillnet were usually beach rocks about the size and shape of a cucumber

150'±   360'

S.F. Manning

Amos Stevens-built Tancook whaler drouging with gillnet.

steel centerboard

Tancook Whaler - 41'0" -
Built by Amos Stevens at Tancook I., Nova Scotia

Measured projection from lines by H.I. Chapelle taken from a half model owned by Ernest A Bell of Halifax, N.S.

Model is believed to represent the final stage of evolution in the working Tancook Whaler

"When the fish would be on quite plenty—herring or mackerel—why, if they got a load they'd have to come in. But ordinary fishing, like cod fishing and pollock and halibut, they would go out on Monday, about one o'clock after dinner, and they'd sail out. They'd have a fairly fresh wind, and they'd pretty well start all at one time. That way they'd be out around sundown."

If a storm threatened while they were out, the fishermen would run for cover wherever they could, depending on the speed and seaworthiness of their whalers to get them to safety. Vernon Langille recalled such an occasion in a forty-footer with no pump in 1904:

"I was only sixteen years old when we got caught in a gale wind out about fifteen miles. . . ."

A large Tancook whaler with washboards to increase carrying capacity lies in a cove in
Lunenburg County in 1915. Maritime Museum of the Atlantic (MMA), Halifax, Nova Scotia

A lapstraked Tancook whaler with wide deck and high coaming is seen
with a load of cargo at Herring Cove, Nova Scotia, in the early 1900s.

"It blew . . . from the east and then it jumped right around to the northwest and it kicked up an awful lot. We were the last boat to leave the ground, and most of them got anywhere from Lunenburg as far up as Shelburne. They skidooed wherever they could get.

"Dad and I stuck to it and beat right into Tancook."

As with boatbuilding, fishing was (and remains) an occupation passed on from generation to generation. This is exemplified in the comments of one interviewee quoted in Kathy Kuusisto's " 'It All Went With Our Living': Life Patterns of Tancook Families." He said, "I fished with my father every summer until he retired. Than I took over. Then we had a

son of our own and he started out, and he fished until I retired. And now, he's taken over."

In addition to fishing, the whalers were also used for coasting, for hauling fish to market at Lunenburg and produce to Halifax and other coastal towns. On their late fall trips, the Tancookers would bring back stores for the winter—flour, sugar, and big boxes of raisins, plus materials for building boats. Mrs. Perry Stevens, Tom Mason's sister, recalls:

"They'd coast this [produce] back and forth. That's where Tom worked very hard and made the living. When my mother and I would stand and look out the window, it would be wintertime—nice and blowy—and he would load the boat. In the bottom would be eggs and sauerkraut and the deck of the vessel would be loaded with half-barrels of sauerkraut. You would see the boat down in the water, and we would think it was sinking.

"My mother would turn her head away and say, 'Oh, my, Tom will be drowned. He'll not make it to Halifax.'

"We would watch the boat going down out of the cove till you could just see something moving. That was the days that we went through hardships, making the living."

* * *

Family bonds needed to be strong on a place like Tancook. If the men had been fishing, everybody turned to when the boats came in. When the catch was herring or mackerel they would be full to within inches of the scuppers. There were no docks, so the fish had to be ferried to the beach in dories. The dories were hauled out and loaded on launches. These launches, also used for hauling the whalers out, consisted of several stringers a yard or so apart, running from below the tide line (seventy to eighty feet or more) to which were spiked crosswise "skidders," spruce logs spaced sixteen to twenty-four inches apart. The stringers rested on old skidders built on the foundations of the previous launch, and perhaps the one before that, with shale stone packed in between.

The skidders were peeled and, as one boatbuilder put it, "slippery as a goose," especially when drenched with cod oil. More recently, crankcase oil was used. But there were no stationary engines on Tancook in the day of the whaler; instead the dories had to be hauled up the launches with oxen or even manually. Rounding up the oxen was up to the women, and sometimes if the oxen were too far afield, men and women worked the capstan together.

If the catch was herring, the women would have to turn to the dressing operation as soon as possible. Mrs. Perry Stevens commented on this "women's work." "If it was 12 or 2 or 3 o'clock in the night, the women dressed the herring. The poor women would have to stand there until the last herring . . . [even] if they'd have six or seven of

those big puncheons [casks]. A woman had to work for her living and those women worked hard."

The herring were dressed at long tables, then washed in puncheons filled with sea water. Sometimes the women would run the dories back down to the shore, filling them with water for washing. After dressing and washing, the fish were salted down in a puncheon. They might be sold right out of this pickle, but more often they were dried because dried fish brought a better price. Pearly Cross, who still runs a store on South East Cove, described how they were dried:

"You'd take them out [of the pickle] and wash them off. Then you'd put them on a heap to press for probably a week. The water would press out of them. They'd take them to the beach and spread them out in the sun to dry. You'd pack them up every night and open them in the morning.

"We used to sell them in Lunenburg, take them by boat to Lunenburg where they'd take them to the West Indies and bring back salt and molasses."

One reason why women dressed herring is that time was critical. As Thomas F. Knight wrote in *Fishes and Fisheries of Nova Scotia*, published in the 1860s, "Herring ought to be gibbed, washed and in pickle, as soon as possible. . . . The flesh being so delicate and tender not only injures quickly by exposure but is much less liable to take the salt." Women and older children also helped with mackerel, but usually not with cod and other groundfish, because these fish were so large and also because it was less essential to get them dressed and salted immediately.

Women often lent a hand when cod were being dried in the fall, however, as they did with smoking. Fish were smoked for home consumption, not commercially. Tom Mason describes the process:

"They'd have a small building, no bottom in it. They'd just make the fire in the center of the building with sawdust. They'd get the fire going and put the sawdust on. That just smoulders and makes smoke. . . . They'd use mostly spruce; the greener it is, the more smoke. If it's too dry, it will burn up and get too hot . . . and cook the fish.

"Before they had smokehouses, they just dug a deep trench, perhaps not under a foot, about 14 feet long, just enough that you could get a good draft up through, a channel for the smoke. . . . They'd take flat rocks and soil (to cover the trench), and the fire would be at one end and a barrel at the other end, where the fish was. You'd have the fish

Tancook whaler being hauled out on slipway.

On Tancook Island at the turn of the century. Note the leather fishing boots.

on rods. A rod would have to be a little longer than the barrel [was wide]. You'd drop it down at an angle and shove it through a hole in the side of the barrel and then bring the other end down and shove it through another hole on the opposite side. . . .

"We put the fish in a weak pickle for probably four to six hours. I think the method they used for making the brine for this was probably when a potato would float. . . . Then they'd take them from there and dry them and then put them in the smokehouse for four or five days. . . . It's something you govern according to your taste."

* * *

Living patterns on Big Tancook, writes Kathy Kuusisto, "were determined by the time of the year and the type of fish caught. A relationship between land and sea had been nurtured over the years and the

work of young and old, men and women alike, was essential to its successful continuation. The dynamic structure of this life cannot be understood by an analysis of fish landings and prices alone." Indeed, it is not easy to get a real feel for what this life was like. The reminiscences of old-timers such as Tom Mason have a ring of truth, of course, and yet their tales are at best childhood recollections and more likely second-hand. People who live on a place like Tancook Island tend not to trouble themselves much with the passage of years—the seasons are far more significant—and so the collective memory can be remarkably imprecise with regard to historical events (recall that some thought there had been whalers in the 1840s, others believed that the first ones dated from about 1880). And for a long time change was not a familiar circumstance on Tancook; social patterns shifted little until the end of the century when the fishing industry picked up, population began to

The Tancook schooner *Oredo* is seen at Volger's Cove, Lunenburg County, in 1904. Built at Lunenburg, she was lapstrake planked, measured 44 feet overall, and grossed 13.6 tons. (MMA)

Blue Rocks, Nova Scotia, in the 1920s showing two transom-sterned Tancook schooners.

Transom-sterned Tancook at
Blue Rocks, Nova Scotia.

A later transom-sterned schooner-yacht in
Halifax, Nova Scotia, showing Tancook
schooner influence.

grow more rapidly, and the island's boatbuilders were busier than ever before.

In 1904, Edwin Pugsley estimated that there was "a fleet of possibly fifty boats [whalers] engaged in fishing and berthed on Tancook, adjacent islands, and the mainland." That would have been as many whalers as there ever were at one time. There were five or six commercial shops on Tancook, plus several builders who sometimes sold new boats to others but were not in business year-round on a commercial basis. In 1911 or 1912, when Tom Mason was five or six—"old enough to remember"—there were two separate commercial operations run by members of the Stevens family, two others run by Reuben Heisler and by Stanley Mason, and a Langille shop. Tom Mason recalled the proprietor of the latter as being Alfred Langille, a testament either to his fitness or to his legendary status on the island, for Al Langille would then have been ninety years old.

Although Tancook's population continued to grow until the eve of World War I, changes elsewhere would have a profound impact. Experiments in the United States in the latter 1880s to develop a safer type of Grand Banks schooner had resulted in a fast and weatherly craft known as the "Fredonia model" which was subsequently built in substantial numbers. The Banks began to yield much larger total catches. Tancookers had no control over what they were paid for fish on the mainland, of course, and larger catches on the Banks eventually sent prices downward. Yields on the Banks were also enhanced as steam power came to the fishing industry; a number of steam trawlers, both wooden and steel, entered the North Atlantic fishery between 1910 and 1918.

On Tancook, one response to the competitive pressure entailed a major change in the design of inshore fishing craft, and it was here that Amos Stevens figured so centrally for his development of the Tancook schooner. A boat with a transom stern had more capacity, of course, but it also had other advantages. As one veteran designer remarked, the whaler proved "too slow in the stays. You couldn't handle them in tight quarters. More fishing, more boats, more fishermen—you needed boats that could spin on a dime."

While the Tancook schooner displaced the whaler, another technological development was starting to loom even larger—internal combustion. Once power became essential to compete, it required capital to get

Cimba, a transom-sterned schooner built by Vernon Langille as a yacht.

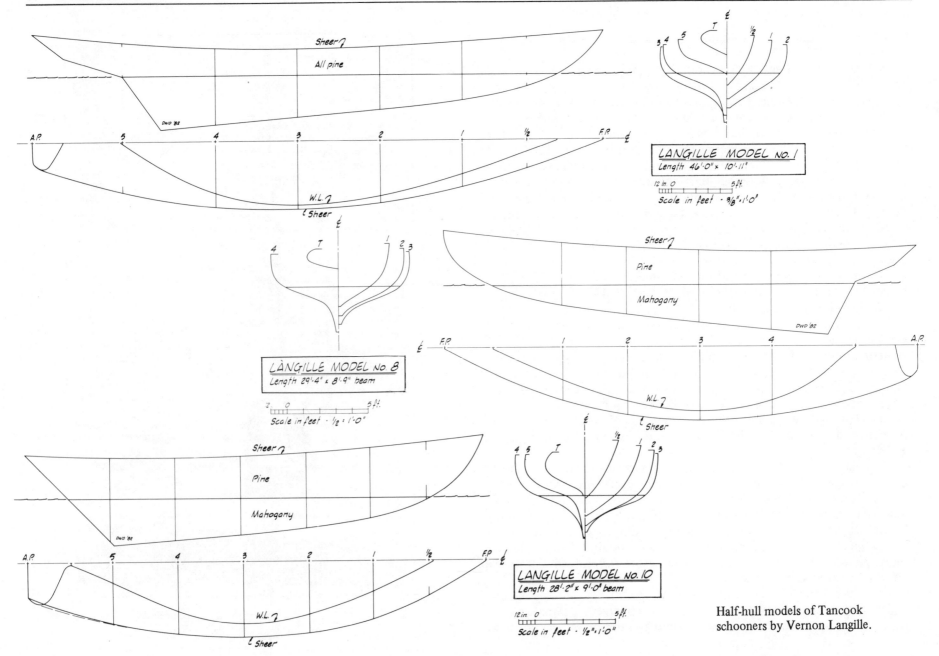

Sheer
All pine

DWD '82

A.P.   5   4   3   2   1   ½   F.P.   ₵

W.L.

Sheer

3 4 5   T   ½   1   2

LANGILLE MODEL No. I
Length 46'·0" x 10'·11"

12 in. 0   5 ft.

Scale in feet · ⅜" · 1'·0"

4   T   1 2 3

LÀNGILLE MODEL No. 8
Length 29'·4" x 8'·9" beam

2   0   5 ft.

Scale in feet · ½ · 1'·0"

Sheer
Pine
Mahogany

DWD '82

₵ F.P.   1   2   3   4   A.P.

W.L.

Sheer

Sheer
Pine
Mahogany

DWD '82

A.P.   5   4   3   2   1   ½   F.P.   ₵

W.L.

Sheer

4 5   T   ½   1 2 3

LANGILLE MODEL No. 10
Length 28'·2" x 9'·0" beam

12 in. 0   5 ft.

Scale in feet · ½" · 1'·0"

Half-hull models of Tancook
schooners by Vernon Langille.

Two views of a 43'6"x 10'8" Tancook whaler
taken by W.S. Archibald in Lunenburg Harbor
on June 25, 1932. (MMA)

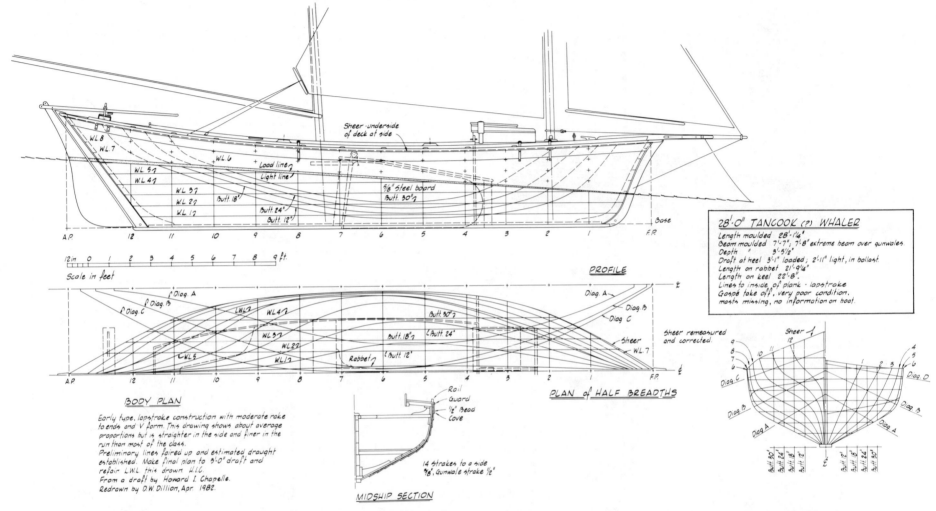

28'-0" TANCOOK (?) WHALER

Length moulded   28'-1¼"
Beam moulded   7'-7½"; 7'-8" extreme beam over gunwales.
Depth   "   3'-5½"
Draft at heel   3'-1" loaded; 2'-11" light, in ballast.
Length on rabbet   21'-9¼".
Length on keel   22'-8".
Lines to inside of plank - lapstrake
Gaspé take off, very poor condition.
masts missing, no information on boat.

PROFILE

BODY PLAN

Early type, lapstrake construction with moderate rake
to ends and V form. This drawing shows about average
proportions but is straighter in the side and finer in the
run than most of the class.
Preliminary lines faired up and estimated draught
established. Make final plan to 3'-0" draft and
refair L.W.L. this drawn. H.I.C.
From a draft by Howard I. Chapelle.
Redrawn by D.W. Dillion, Apr. 1982.

MIDSHIP SECTION

Rail
Guard
½" Bead
Cove

14 strakes to a side
⅝", Gunwale strake ½"

PLAN of HALF BREADTHS

into the inshore fishing industry. Since Tancook Islanders rarely had capital, the fishing industry peaked and the exodus began. Among those to leave the island after the war were all of the old-time boatbuilders.

The Tancook whaler was becoming scarce even in the 1920s (which explains why Howard Chapelle's discovery of the Middle River boat in 1948 was quite an event). Yet the type had not dropped from sight altogether, for the Stevenses and other former Tancook Island builders kept with the design on the mainland in the 1930s, and it was being copied by yacht designers in the United States as well. Although the purists would always contend that these boats "were not really whalers," they did provide a link to the present and provide part of the impetus that ultimately resulted in construction of the *Vernon Langille*. And so we turn again from Tancook Island to the Tancook whaler.

PART II

3 Connections

When Ernest Bell indicated in 1933 that the Tancook whaler was on the verge of extinction, strictly speaking he was correct, for there were no more traditional whalers in use as workboats. Yet whalers were still being built on Mahone Bay by former Tancook Islanders. And at least one of these had found its way to the United States. In 1927, William Lee of Harwichport, Massachusetts, purchased a forty-one-foot Tancook Island original named *Evangeline* at Chester, a boat that had likely been built by a Stevens or a Mason. Two years later, Lee sold her to George Blenkhorn, a Nova Scotian living on Cape Cod who liked her familiar lines. Blenkhorn renamed her *Whistling Cat.* Later he decked her over, added power, and changed the rig, and she remained serviceable until after World War II.

More important to the perpetuation of the type, however, was this: Lee had taken off *Evangeline*'s lines, and in 1931, working from a design of Walter Cross, he built a thirty-foot whaler named *Wind Dog*. A year or two later an incident took place that was remarkably similar to the one recounted by Ernest Bell. This time the narrator was Ralph Wiley, the boatbuilder from Oxford, Maryland. Wiley was involved in a race of sorts, aboard a fifty-foot schooner reaching toward Vineyard Haven. Then it happened:

"Out of Robinson's Hole appeared a tiny thirty-foot double-end schooner, a Tancook whaler. Her course converged with ours. When abeam her skipper, puffing contentedly on a corncob pipe and wearing a derby hat at a jaunty angle, stepped forward, 'wung' out the foresail, and proceeded to leave us behind. By the time we reached harbor the derby-crowned skipper had anchored, furled his sails and gone ashore."

Wiley and a friend rowed over to inspect this "smart little vessel," which of course was *Wind Dog*. Shortly afterward, the friend bought her, and, following a fast outside passage from Boston to the Virginia Capes, she put in to Wiley's boatyard on Chesapeake Bay, where he was able to study her closely. Attuned more to yachts than workboats, Wiley reported that "*Wind Dog* was without nearly everything." There was no engine, head, or galley; ballast consisted of boiler punchings. But, he added, "her hull lines were beautiful, and when her loose-footed foresail was sheeted to overlap the mainsail she certainly could sail."

"With *Wind Dog* as an incentive," Wiley wrote in his autobiography, "I designed and built five whalers. The general proportions of beam and profile were similar, but the bilges were hardened, the ballast placed outside and a modern jib-headed cutter rig replaced the schooner rig." The first was a thirty-one-footer named *Mocking Bird* which Wiley kept himself, racing her on the Bay until 1956. A thirty-eight-footer built in 1944 won the annual Annapolis-to-Oxford race in 1962. Roger Taylor, the eminent connoisseur of good boats, writes that "Wiley appears to have achieved something which is most difficult: the intelligent modification of a working craft into a yacht. Some of us might still prefer to sail the original Tancook whaler," Taylor continues, "but the choice here is really a matter of taste, not a question of selecting good over bad."

By the 1960s vessels with some resemblance to Tancook whalers had been designed in Connecticut by Howard Chapelle's friend George Stadel and built at such points on the Maine coast as Owls Head and

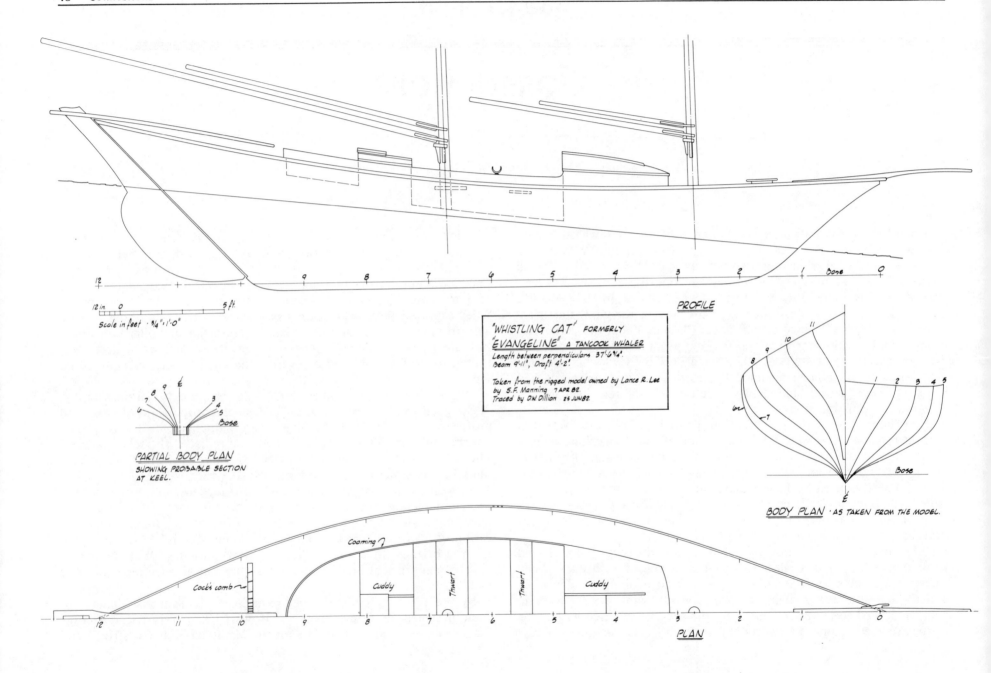

PROFILE

12 in. 0   5 ft.
Scale in feet · ¾" : 1'·0"

"WHISTLING CAT" FORMERLY
"EVANGELINE" A TANCOOK WHALER
Length between perpendiculars 37'·6¾'.
Beam 9'·11", Draft 4'·2'

Taken from the rigged model owned by Lance R. Lee
by S.F. Manning   7 APR 82.
Traced by D.W. Dillion 26 JUN 82.

PARTIAL BODY PLAN
SHOWING PROBABLE SECTION
AT KEEL.

BODY PLAN · AS TAKEN FROM THE MODEL.

Coaming

Cock's comb   Cuddy   Thwart   Thwart   Cuddy

PLAN

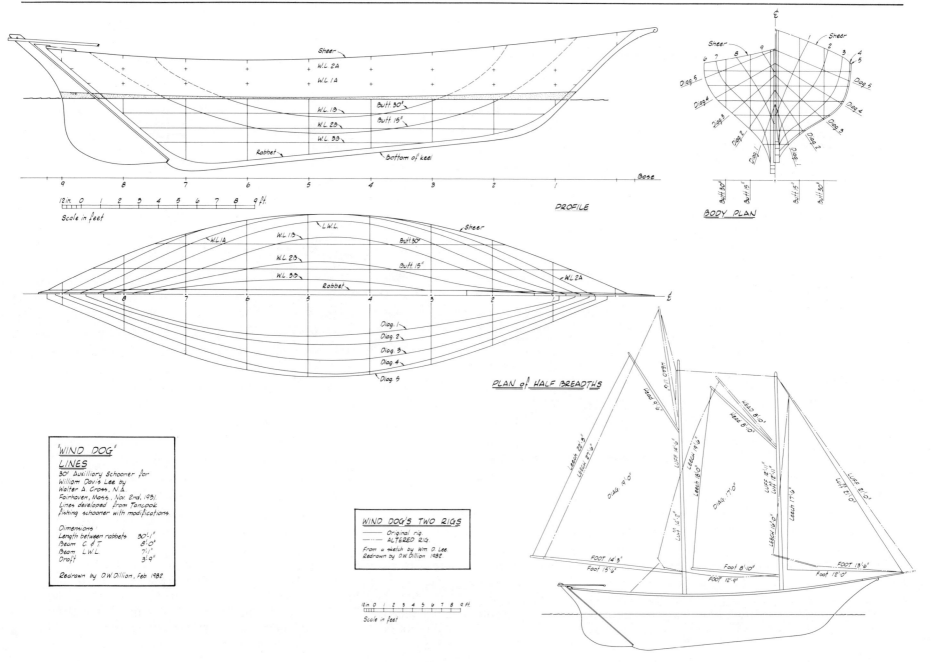

Sheer
W.L. 2A
W.L. 1A
W.L. 1B   Butt. 30"
W.L. 2B   Butt. 15"
W.L. 3B
Rabbet
Bottom of keel
Base

Scale in feet
12 in. 0 1 2 3 4 5 6 7 8 9 ft.

PROFILE

Sheer
9
6 7 8
Diag. 5
Diag. 4
Diag. 3
Diag. 2
Diag. 1
Butt. 30" Butt. 15" Butt. 15" Butt. 30"

1
Sheer
2
3
4
5
Diag. 5
Diag. 4
Diag. 3
Diag. 2

BODY PLAN

W.L. 1A   W.L. 1B   L.W.L.   Butt. 30"   Sheer
W.L. 2B   Butt. 15"
W.L. 3B
Rabbet   W.L. 2A

Diag. 1
Diag. 2
Diag. 3
Diag. 4
Diag. 5

PLAN of HALF BREADTHS

"WIND DOG"
LINES
30' Auxilliary Schooner for
William Davis Lee by
Walter A. Cross, N.A.
Fairhaven, Mass., Nov. 2nd, 1931.
Lines developed from Tancook
fishing schooner with modifications.

Dimensions
Length between rabbets   30'-1"
Beam C & T   8'-0"
Beam L.W.L.   7'-1"
Draft   3'-9"

Redrawn by D.W.Dillion, Feb. 1982.

WIND DOG'S TWO RIGS
——— Original rig.
–·–·– ALTERED RIG.

From a sketch by Wm. O. Lee.
Redrawn by D.W. Dillion 1982.

Scale in feet
12 in. 0 1 2 3 4 5 6 7 8 9 Ft.

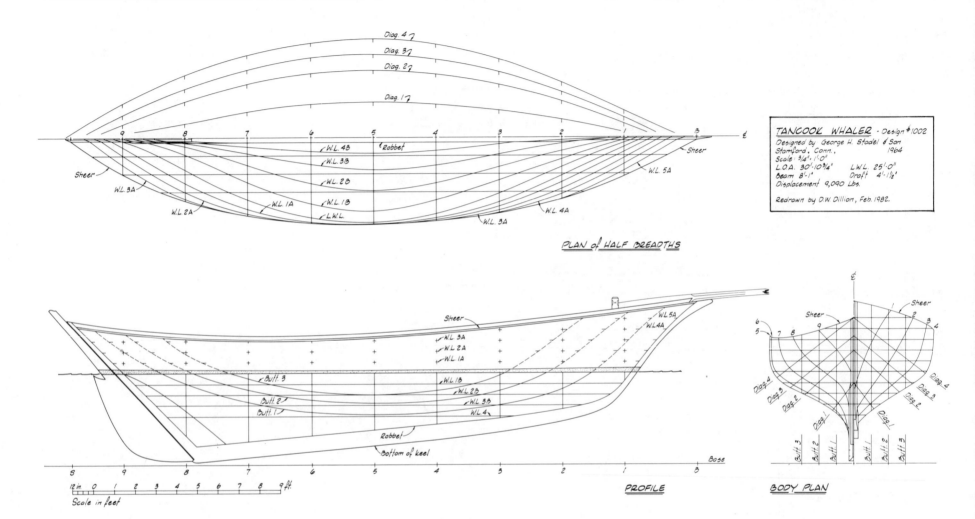

TANCOOK WHALER - Design #1002
Designed by George H. Stadel & Son
Stamford, Conn.,   1964
Scale: 3/4", 1'-0"
L.O.A. 30'-10¾"   L.W.L. 25'-0"
Beam 8'-1"   Draft 4'-1½'
Displacement 9,090 Lbs.

Redrawn by D.W. Dillion, Feb. 1982.

PLAN of HALF BREADTHS

Scale in feet

PROFILE   BODY PLAN

Boothbay Harbor—Stadel once insisted that "the last Tancooker" was built in 1964 by Boothbay's Chet Rittall. And since the 1970s *National Fisherman* has carried features on whalers built in such unlikely places as Hornby Island (British Columbia) and Houston. In most instances the builders have paid explicit homage to Chapelle's lines, and yet the purists always protest that these craft are not "true" whalers. "When they take them and add heavy materials and high freeboard and build interiors and heavy lead keels, then of course they're not a whaler by any means," declared one of the Stevenses. In some cases, the anomalies of a "modern" whaler can be disconcerting. For example, an

A 46-foot Crocker-designed Tancook schooner yacht adaptation in frame. Note that the method of building which employed frame molds was used.

Annapolis builder, Peter Van Dine, has built twenty-five- and thirty-five-foot whalers with a hull shape that (in Taylor's words) "a Tancook Islander would have been proud of"—hulls that are molded in fiberglass.

The choice, as Taylor points out, is a matter of taste, not quality. On the one hand are those who value tradition above all; on the other, those who appreciate some measure of comfort. The disagreement cannot be resolved, though it is worth noting that any modification of the traditional design has entailed trade-offs. Even the *Evangeline*, William

Lee's son Lance noted, had had her centerboard removed and a keel added, hence could no longer operate in shoal waters. The *Laura S*, a whaler designed by Sam Crocker and built at the Lee yard in the late 1930s, drew seven feet of water. In meeting the demands of yachtsmen, the primary loss is in flexibility. The building of one traditional Tancook whaler—among all those that have diverged from tradition to an appreciable degree—was, then, a project worthwhile in the doing, and, we trust, doubly worthwhile in the recounting.

4 A Whaler Takes Shape in Bath

In the summer of 1977, the Maine Maritime Museum's Apprentice-shop applied to the National Endowment for the Arts for a grant to cover costs of researching and building a traditional Tancook whaler. Lance Lee, the shop's director, was particularly interested in the whaler because of his father's role in introducing the type to the United States. Two of the apprentices, Mark Swanson and Joe Postich, were likewise specially interested. "One particular boat—the Tancook whaler—had fascinated me since my arrival at the shop," Joe recalled. "There were pictures of her everywhere, and a beautiful model. I wanted to do something. . . ."

One evening in October Joe and Mark were working late, when Joe suddenly called, "Hey, Mark, how would you like to loft the whaler?"

Mark Swanson needed no urging. He had been intrigued by the lines of the Middle River boat in Howard Chapelle's *American Small Sailing Craft* and was eager to draw out those lines full-scale on the lofting floor. The two apprentices completed this task in short order, then, shortly afterward, the good news arrived from Washington—the NEA had authorized the grant.

* * *

While drawing out Chapelle's lines had been a useful exercise, actually building a forty-footer would have been too ambitious an undertaking. The initial proposal had been conceived with a twenty-eight-footer in mind, and in truth nobody was quite sure yet what version of the whaler they should build. Nor were they sure of how to proceed. It seemed essential to commence the project by visiting the source—going to Tancook Island and the Mahone Bay mainland and seeking out people who knew the original craft at first hand.

In David Stevens's boatshop at Second Peninsula, Lance, Joe, and Mark imbibed the techniques of the old-time Tancook boatbuilders. Stevens showed them the method of setting up steam-bent frame molds, taking lines from a half-model, and other techniques passed on by his grandfather, Amos. More important, Stevens reinforced their enthusiasm for getting on with the job. Here he was, retired and in his eighties, almost singlehandedly building a forty-foot schooner, teaching his grandson as he went. When told that Chapelle's forty-foot whaler would be too big for the Apprenticeshop, he replied: "My God, man, knock the walls down!"

From Stevens, and from Tom Mason, the visitors from Maine also imbibed some of the competitive spirit of the Nova Scotians. Mason excitedly described races around the island that tested the new boats each spring, and contests against boats from the mainland. When questioned about the relative merits of different whaler models, he became convinced that the objective was to build a boat to beat the Canadians in their annual International Schooner Races at nearby St. Margarets Bay. "Boy, it's coming out now," he said. "I knew there was something in this. Take the cup back to the States. . . ."

Stevens fired up the imagination of the visitors, but the ultimate inspiration came when they went to the shop of Vernon Langille, dean of Nova Scotia builders and the man to whom all others ultimately deferred for the final word on the old whalers and how they were made. Joe Postich wrote in his journal: "We all walked over to Vernon's shop with great anticipation. I didn't believe it. Here in front of my eyes

52

Amos Stevens of Tancook Island in 1907 with
one of his half-hull models.

Vernon Langille at Indian Point, Lunenburg
County, Nova Scotia, at age 85 in 1973. (MMA)

Vernon Langille's shop as photographed by George Stadel during a visit in the 1930s. The method of building using steam-bent frame molds is evident, as is the stem rabbet cut for each plank just before it goes on.

loomed the whole contemporary history of Nova Scotia boatbuilding. All of us became charged, including Mr. Langille. This 91-year-old man who had been struggling to walk seemed to glide up into his mold loft. . . ."

* * *

Early in their sojourn to Mahone Bay the trio from the Apprenticeshop reached two key decisions: that their whaler would be a scaled-down version of Chapelle's 40-foot Middle River boat (she ultimately measured 34'-8" on deck), and that she would be directly lofted from the half-model in accord with the practice of the early builders on Tancook Island, a practice still followed by David Stevens and other traditionalists (including some contemporary lobsterboat builders along the Maine coast).

From the start, Chapelle's lines had appealed to the Apprenticeshop crew. Subsequent to the First World War, even whalers built on Mahone Bay had ordinarily been fitted with a keel rather than a centerboard. They were like all the other whalers built in the United States as pleasure boats, modified to meet the demands of yachtsmen, gaining something but losing in flexibility. Now, the aim was to get back to a simply constructed boat, shoal-draft, low-freeboard, fast, light, and able.

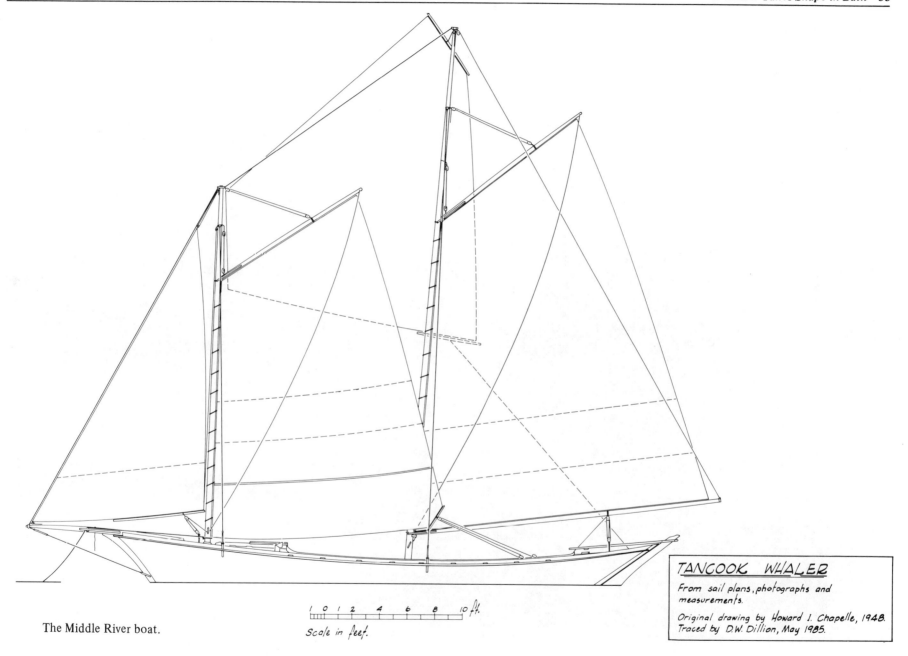

The Middle River boat.

1 0 1 2 4 6 8 10 ft.

Scale in feet.

TANCOOK WHALER

From sail plans, photographs and measurements.

Original drawing by Howard I. Chapelle, 1948.
Traced by D.W. Dillion, May 1985.

The Middle River boat, the whaler from which Howard Chapelle took the lines in 1948. The vessel was built about 1905-1910 and measured 40'x 9'8"x 4'2". (MMA)

Model of a Tancook whaler posed against a backdrop of the Kennebec River and a perspective drawing by Howard Chapelle.

In 1931 Amos Stevens, then retired, had carved a half-model for Ernest Bell, and it was from this that Chapelle had taken the lines which accompanied Bell's article on "The Passing of the Tancook Whaler." But the lines of the Middle River boat were finer, suggesting greater speed, and in the end the Apprenticeshop went with this later set of Chapelle lines. As for construction technique, the visitors from

Bath had been impressed by the simple cost-saving method of designing with a half-model and then lofting directly from the model. As David Stevens put it:

"I can glue a piece of wood together and in two hours I can have a half-model made for a 45-foot schooner. In a couple more hours, I can have the lines down and ready to go to work. For a blueprint, you have

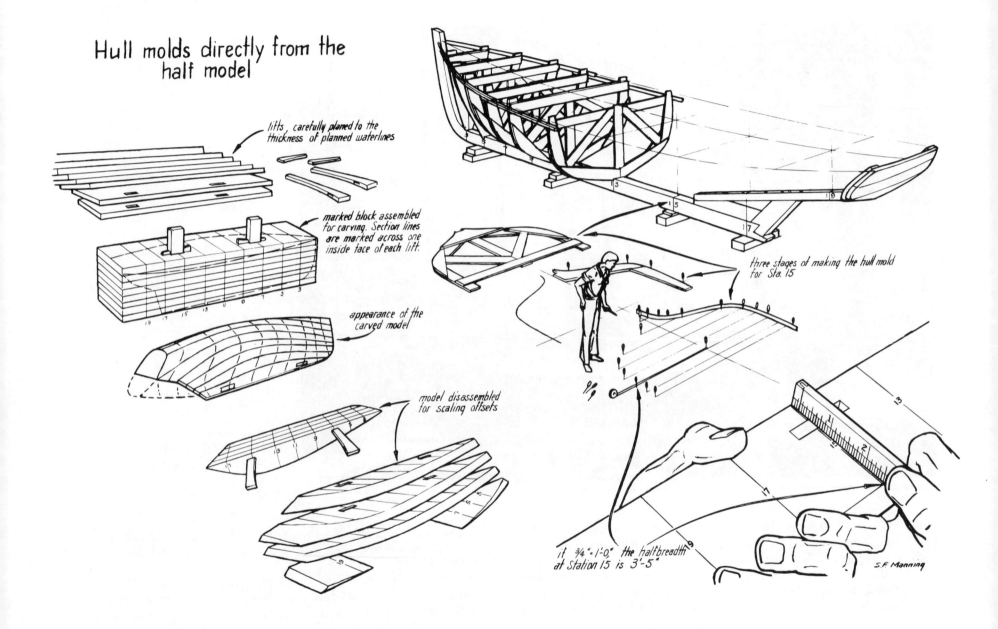

Hull molds directly from the half model

lifts, carefully planed to the thickness of planned waterlines

marked block assembled for carving. Section lines are marked across one inside face of each lift.

appearance of the carved model

model disassembled for scaling offsets

three stages of making the hull mold for Sta. 15

it 3/4"=1'-0" the halfbreadth at Station 15 is 3'-5"

S.F. Manning

to have a naval architect draw it for you. And then by the time you have it puzzled out and lofted and so on, I can have the boat set up and planked—almost; maybe not quite."

Mark Swanson, a gifted woodworker, had been making half-models ever since his arrival at the Apprenticeshop nine months before. He had, in fact, already carved a model of Chapelle's forty-footer. The problem was to reduce this by five feet or so. The lines could not merely be shrunk proportionately without sacrificing some of the seakeeping capability of the original craft.

Upon returning to Maine, the apprentices sought the advice of Jay Paris, a Bath naval architect and Museum trustee. Paris saw a solution in shrinking the ends while leaving the beam and draft the same as Chapelle's lines. This would enhance stability and provide the working space desirable in a vessel to be used for sail training. Under Paris's guidance, Mark went to work on a new half-model. In his own words, this is how he proceeded:

"Chapelle's half-breadths were taken up and faired onto paper on stations spaced 21 inches, rather than 24 inches. This reduction (12 percent, or roughly 1/8" for every 1" real scale) brought both stem and stern more upright and obviously increased her beam to length ratio, bringing her shape more to that of whalers fishing in the early 1900s.

"The carving, then, to 3/4"=1' scale of a model of our Tancook's starboard side—this became my task. My knees still shake and my head spins as I consider the audacity of my effort to give a boat shape, rather arbitrarily, without a lifetime of boatbuilding and boat handling to guide me.

"Following Chapelle's station shapes between stations two and fourteen was pretty simple. The greatest difficulty there was fairing the keel taper. At either end, the curve of the sheer in half-breadth faired to look rather Viking-like as I followed Chapelle's lines on our shorter framework, so I allowed my sense of sight and touch to govern the shape during the carving. I carved the ends fair, giving them more fullness and making them slightly more plumb than those of Mr. Chapelle. A tremendous amount of care was taken to ensure that the edge of the model at the ends was to scale—1" in reality, 1/16" on the model. This was a spot I reworked repeatedly to get it right, as getting it right was the whole point.

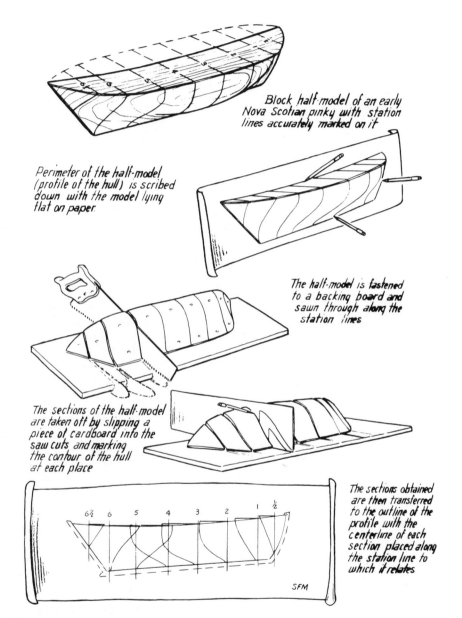

Block half-model of an early Nova Scotian pinky with station lines accurately marked on it

Perimeter of the half-model (profile of the hull) is scribed down with the model lying flat on paper.

The half-model is fastened to a backing board and sawn through along the station lines

The sections of the half-model are taken off by slipping a piece of cardboard into the saw cuts and marking the contour of the hull at each place

The sections obtained are then transferred to the outline of the profile with the centerline of each section placed along the station line to which it relates

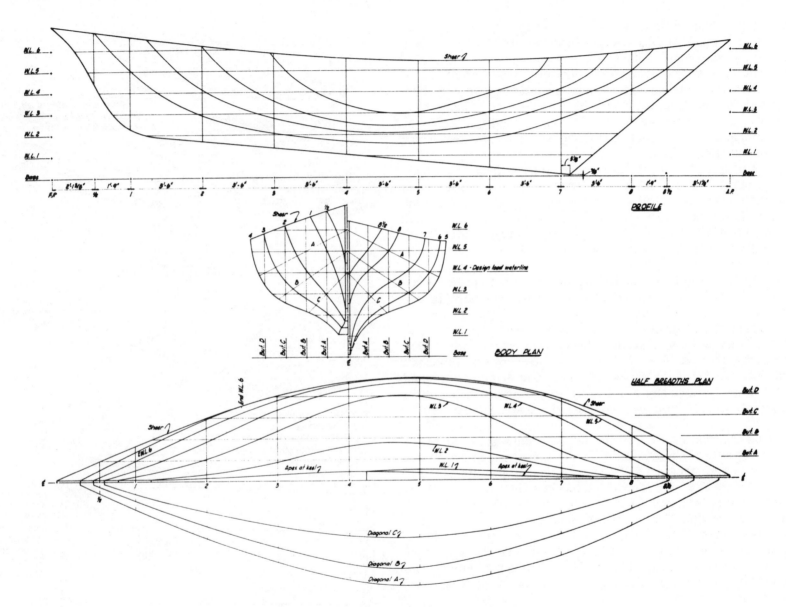

Early lines plan of the Apprenticeshop's Tancook whaler.

"I took the model to Jay Paris, who looked it over very carefully. Comparing it to photographs of Mahone Bay Tancooks, we decided to increase the sternpost-to-deck angle from the 30 degrees I had carved to a 33-degree angle more closely approximating the whalers lined up on the shore in an old Tancook Island photograph. This process removed one foot from the deck length and introduced a fuller set of curves to the stern section. Mr. Paris, by the way, found my fairing sound and perfectly reasonable, which was a great surprise and relief to me."

* * *

With the half-model completed and approved by the professional advisor, it was time to begin lofting. Joe continues his account:

"Our first job was to transfer the lines of the model to the scaleboard. The half-model was laid down flat on a clear piece of cedar and the profile marked all around, along with the station lines and the waterline. Chapelle's 40-footer was drawn to the inner rabbet line, and we kept ours the same. Our profile below the sheer was bounded by the middle line of the rabbet.

"Once the stations and waterline were drawn in, the beam and keel widths were measured at each station on the model and transferred to the board. We used two methods to lift off the section shapes for the body plan. Mark made templates to fit at each station. I molded an architect's lead bar to the shape of the hull at the stations. The bar, which retains its shape, is then laid on the profile at the station and scribed out.

"The simplicity of this overwhelmed me. I didn't believe it could be so easy, so I would gingerly pick up the lead and hold it back against the model to see if it had changed shape, then take it back to the board for a final check. We also had Mark's templates for confirmation."

Using a scale rule, measurements from the scaleboard were then transferred full-size to plywood and painted flat white, with baseline and waterlines drawn on at one-foot intervals. Again following a technique observed in Nova Scotia, the apprentices lofted their body plan on both sides of the centerline to facilitate steam-bending of 7/8" x 3" white oak stock which was to be used for the molds.

* * *

Master Builder Dave Foster explains method of transferring lines from the half model to the scale board.

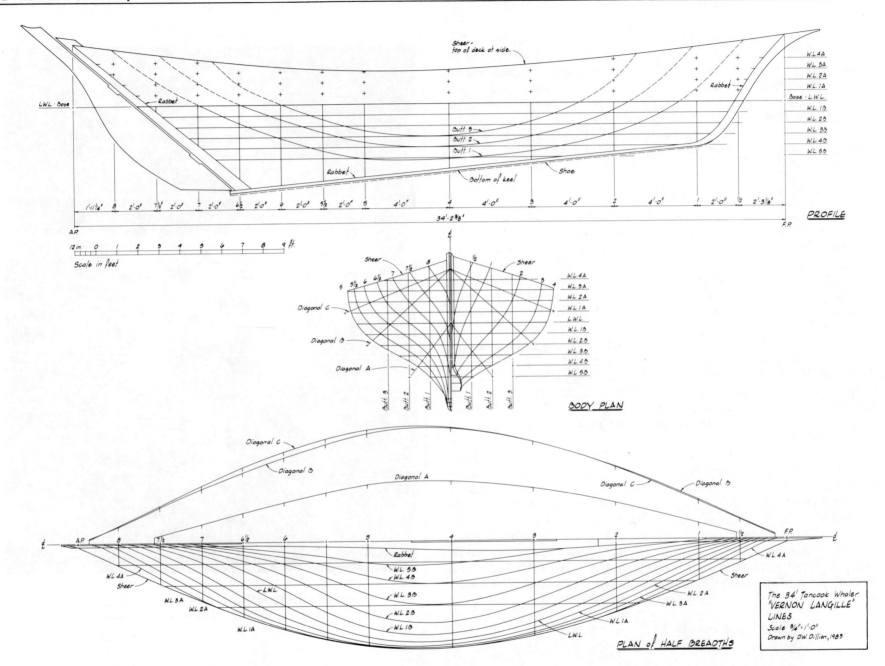

PROFILE

Scale in feet

BODY PLAN

PLAN of HALF BREADTHS

The 34' Tancook Whaler
"VERNON LANGILLE"
LINES
Scale 3/4" = 1'-0"
Drawn by D.W. Dillion, 1983

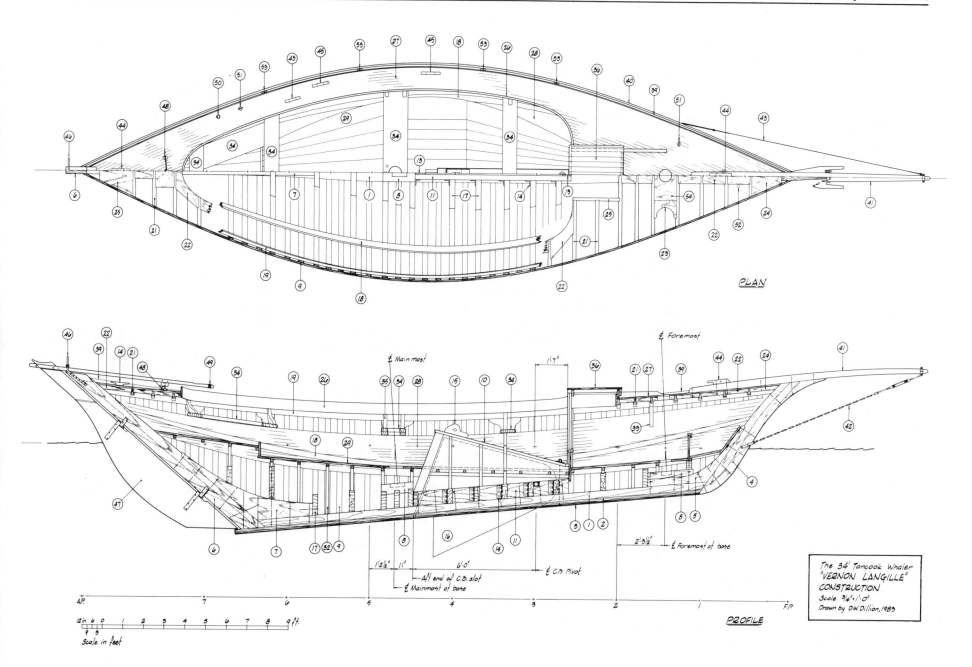

PLAN

€ Main mast

€ Foremast

1'-7"

€ Foremast of base

€ C.B. Pivot

Aft end of C.B. slot

€ Mainmast at base

1'-2½"   1'-0"

6'-0"

2'-3½"

A.P.   7   6   5   4   3   2   1   F.P.

PROFILE

12 in. 6 0   1   2   3   4   5   6   7   8   9 ft.
      9 3

Scale in feet

The 34' Tancook Whaler
"VERNON LANGILLE"
CONSTRUCTION
Scale ¾"=1'-0"
Drawn by D.W. Dillion, 1983

Then it was time to start building. Master Builder Dave Foster, busy with other shop tasks, left the apprentices largely to figure things out for themselves. Donn Costanzo, who was shortly to join Mark and Joe, recalls:

"At the beginning stage of each process, one would read Chapelle's *Boatbuilding,* then try to interpret and relate it to the specific problem. If we got stumped, we went to Dave and tactfully asked him to explain it. A lot of questions Joe and Mark and I would discuss at great length, and I found this to be one of the greatest assets in the learning process—simply talking out the problem with your coworkers."

Foster gives full credit to the apprentices. "It was seat of the pants all the way," he says, "three greenhorns with only one boat each behind them. It was their enthusiasm that did it."

The first job was making the steam-bent molds, a new experience for the Apprenticeshop. Though the process was supposed to save time, the apprentices were unsure of how to proceed. At first, they believed that the molds were to become part of the boat, thereby saving labor and wood. But when confronted with the problem of beveling them, they decided to call David Stevens in Nova Scotia. Stevens's word was to take the molds out after framing was completed. One advantage of these steam-bent oak molds was that they provided excellent holding for screws to fasten the ribbands.

The molds, sixteen of them for eight stations, were steamed and bent together with horizontal spalls at the sheer and keel, a big vertical brace down the center, and diagonals from the waterline to the center brace.

* * *

With all molds bent and spalled, the apprentices turned to the backbone. Although Chapelle reported that the keel of the Middle River boat appeared to be birch, descendents of the old-time Tancook builders indicated that oak was more commonly used. Some beautiful 2-inch oak had been donated to the shop, and the keel—22'x4"x7¼" maximum—was made up from two layers of this stock, scarfed, bedded in 5200, and joined by 3/8" galvanized bolts. The Nova Scotians called this plank keel a "bottom." The Apprenticeshop's whaler was designed with a 7/8" centerboard slot 83½" long, extending from 3-3/4" aft of station 3 to 3-1/2 inches aft of station 5. Half-inch bolts fore and aft of the slot prevented splitting.

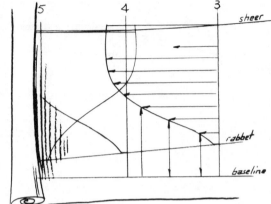

Sections of the hull laid out on the outline of the model's profile constitute a plan or lines-draught which can be scaled.

Curve of the hull at each station where the model was cut can be scaled from the draught by measurements taken inward to the station line (#3) and downward to a measurement baseline drawn beneath the keel.

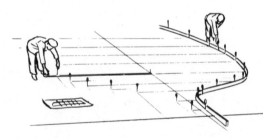

Here's Section 3 laid out in full size on a loft floor. The sectional curve is laid out for both sides of the boat with measured offsets taken to the centerline and the baseline.

A batten is bent smoothly around picks stuck into the location marks.

The curve is pencilled on to the floor.

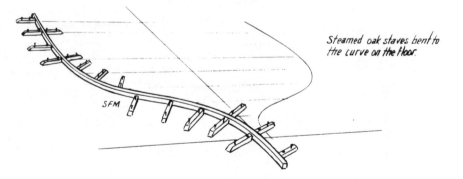

Steamed oak staves bent to the curve on the floor.

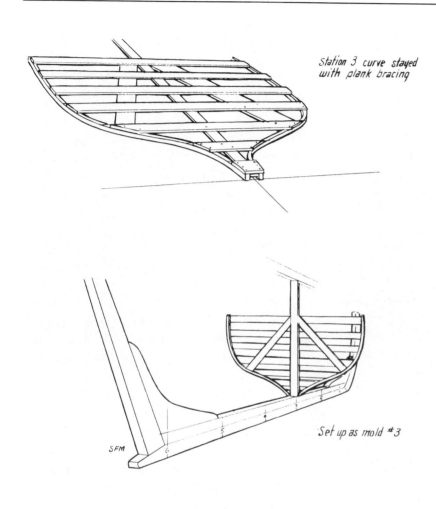

Station 3 curve stayed with plank bracing

SFM

Set up as mold #3

Building the stem-bent molds on the body plan drawn on the floor.

Laying out of the after section keel pattern on two-inch oak stock.

The tapered oak keel showing the two-inch stock bedded together and fastened with through bolts. The centerboard slot can also be seen.

The keel had no rabbets. Rather, the frames fit flush against its upper sides and bevels received the garboards. Later, the apprentices trimmed the garboards and added another two-inch piece of keel to cover the ends. (Although it was not in the plans, a work shoe was also added, a standard feature of all boats built by the Apprenticeshop.) "The thing about that keel," Dave Foster recalled, "is that it made fitting the garboards a lot easier, because you just let the garboards run wild down there. . . . we planed them off afterward."

* * *

Back at the loft, patterns were made for the stem and sternpost using Chapelle's scantlings. The inner rabbet was marked from the profile on the scaleboard. The patterns lacked rabbets and bending lines, and these were obtained by taking bevels directly from the half-model, the bevels being transferred to a board and then to the stem and sternpost after these had been cut out and the inner rabbet marked.

The original Tancook builders had used one large natural crook for both stem and knee. As there was no piece of white oak available that was long enough for the sternpost, two pieces were scarfed together. And in the absence of a suitable natural crook, Joe Postich laminated a big stem knee from many pieces of straight-grained white oak. He tells something of what this entailed:

"Despite objections from experts who say you can't glue oak, it seems to have worked perfectly. Of course, keel bolts acted as omnipresent clamps for the knee, but even before she was bolted the knee showed no signs of delamination. The gluing process goes something like this. . . .

"Make a form approximating the shape you want. Steal some waxed paper from the kitchen, so your epoxied pieces won't stick to the bench. Get a lot of cold-weather epoxy, about 20 clamps, and the driest white oak you can find. Seasoned oak is essential.

"Now, cut up as many half-inch strips of oak as you need with the correct siding plus an eighth-inch. Do not plane; rough surfaces give better adhesion, and epoxy will fill gaps up to a sixteenth-inch and doesn't require tight fits like other glues. Mix your glue, armed with vapor mask and gloves, and put a light skim coat on each of the gliding surfaces.

Stem piece assembly showing the laminated stem knee.

"By the way, cut out more pieces of oak than the shape calls for so the pattern can be placed most advantageously, and heed the amount of time the manufacturer specifies for mixing the glue. The folks at T-88 say three minutes. That doesn't seem long, but I timed it, and I had never approached that length of time in mixing before. I noted that the texture had changed somewhat from what I had been getting with my normal minute or two."

After applying the skim coat and waiting overnight, the epoxied pieces were sanded rough to the touch and wiped off. Then a good-sized batch of glue was mixed and the pieces coated. Donn continues:

"We had left some long pieces of oak sticking out past the rest at intervals so we could clamp them to the form. We clamped about five at a time, shifting clamps where necessary and also using bar clamps. . . . By the way, don't clamp too tightly or you'll squeeze all the glue out. About 10-15 pounds is good. . . .

"The next day, plane or sand major globs off your wood and send it through a thickness planer for final siding. It actually looks very nice now, so put your pattern on it and cut it on the bandsaw."

* * *

The centerboard and centerboard trunk were objects of considerable controversy. While Dave Foster was confident that Chapelle's scantlings would work fine, some shop visitors were skeptical. "Experts poured in like leaves in October," Joe observed. In fact, even Chapelle had had doubts about the centerboard design—a distinctive feature of the Tancook originals—noting the "poor shape" which he thought would strain the case when the centerboard was lowered. But Dave Foster did not share these misgivings. He made the structure stronger by attaching the trunk to the floor timbers with 3x3 angle irons which Mark had located in a scrapyard and then had cut, drilled, and sent to Quincy, Massachusetts, for galvanizing. The board itself was fabricated of stainless steel donated by Bath Iron Works.

"I've thought a lot about that centerboard," said Foster. "Many boats have a centerboard that is entirely under the cabin floor, which would also mean a very narrow board. Our board is narrow only on the forward end; it's real wide on the after end. I don't think it was ever intended that the after part of the board should come out of the slot. The

Starting to cut the stem rabbet.

pennant should be the right length so that you've always got a lot of it up in there. I think the design of that was real clever."

In service, the board has proven trouble-free, and the triangular shape a boon to crews loading cargo because it allows more freedom of movement athwartships in the forward part of the cockpit. The original fisherman-builders probably had this in mind.

The centerboard case was made from materials salvaged from an abandoned railroad building in Portland. The bedlogs were 4x6 pieces of what Joe called "the most seasoned white oak you ever saw." These were rabbeted inside to accept 3/4" longleaf yellow pine planks, also from the railroad building, spiled together with white pine. The head ledges and cap were of white oak.

*   *   *

After the Apprenticeshop trio had placed the keel on a strongback and bolted stem and sternpost in place, they turned to setting up the molds. Beginning with number 4 and initially working forward, the molds were cleated to the keel. In customary fashion, the forward molds were set aft of the station lines, the after molds forward of the stations. After being plumbed and braced aft, they were horned with more braces aft, then leveled. Once established in this three-dimensional space, the molds were braced to the shop ceiling, across the boat to contract the stresses of the ribbanding process. Each subsequent mold was braced to the previous one as well as to the ceiling, thereby establishing an extremely strong structure, and one already quite fair.

Indeed, the fairness of the whaler's skeleton was a surprise to all hands, especially to Dave Foster, who had warned the apprentices that as ribbanding began they could expect to have a lot of fairing to do. Joe described his own apprehensions: "Inwardly, I wonder if any of the molds will line up at all, much less fair nicely into the stem and sternpost rabbets which have courageously been cut with little to spare. I can't bear to watch as Dave starts wrapping ribbands around the hull. . . . "

Joe need not have been so concerned: "The ribbands seem to fit perfectly on the molds and actually end up in the rabbets—at both ends, no less. There's much celebration at our bench. Dave can't quite believe it. There's no way I can get the grin off my face. I don't know or care

about anything but the whaler. I feel a sense of life in her for the first time. . . ."

The ribbands were cut from rather heavy stock—2x2 spruce—and there had been some speculation that these moved some of the molds as they were bent on. But Foster points out that everything was well braced, with little give.

Like the molds, the frames that were next steamed and bent into place were 7/8"x3" oak, canoe frames spaced on 1/8" centers, 120 in all. They were cut and beveled before steaming, and screw-fastened to the keel.

Chapelle's scantlings called for 7/8" spruce or pine planking. The Apprenticeshop's whaler was to be planked with Maine cedar, however —not as strong as spruce or pine—so 1-1/8" boards were used. They also were narrower than Nova Scotia practice because, as Foster put it, "Maine cedar doesn't grow very wide and what's wide isn't very good." To add longitudinal strength, 1-3/8" white oak was used for the sheer strakes and garboards. Fastenings were 1-1/2" #12 silicon-bronze flathead woodscrews; sheer strakes were bolted with bronze carriage bolts. "Those thin frames would have been better clench-nailed," Foster says, "but you just can't get good clench nails. I think the one thing I'd do differently would be to rivet her with copper rivets."

Even though the job generally went smoothly, planking up a Tancook whaler was not as easy for these apprentices as it would have been for David Stevens. Donn Costanzo recalls spending about four days at Christmas 1978 in sub-zero weather fitting the after port garboard by himself. But there were compensations. After about five planks had been bent on down from the sheer, the apprentices turned to what Donn later called "the most beautiful single unit in the boat"—the floor timbers.

These were placed every third frame for most of the boat, every other frame at the centerboard trunk, and every one of the three frames under the mainmast step. Not being able to obtain the traditional long natural crooks—called "hooks" by the Nova Scotians—they used three-inch longleaf yellow pine, which had been salvaged from that ninety-year-old railroad building in Portland, too. After these were fitted on top of the frames and bedded, they were fastened with five #16 three-inch flathead bronze wood-screws through the frame into the pine end grain. Later, after the garboards were in place and the first shoe fitted,

Setting up the forward frame-molds.

The backbone assembly from port side, aft, showing the first bent of frame-molds set up.

Fastening ribbands to the frame-molds
in preparation for framing.

Running the sheer batten over the frame-molds.

Above, forward frames are bent to the battens and fastened; right, midsection frames are bent to the battens.

Planking: the oak sheer strake has already been
fitted as apprentices begin planking the hull.

Maine cedar 1-1/8" was used for planking.

The 1-3/8" white oak starboard garboard is
fitted and fastened at the stem.

Overall port-side view of the planking.

Fitting frames to receive planking.

Cutting the end of the shutter or last plank on the hull.

Fitting the shutter plank.

the floor timbers also were bolted to the keel, greatly strengthening the bond between frames and keel.

Not that the apprentices found it easy to fit the floor timbers. "Foster's way," Mark recalled, "was to lay a piece of pattern board against the wider side of the frames, then the inside edges of the frames were scribed to the board. Along these lines (the frame-side of the timbers), three or four marks were made perpendicular to the curve of the frame and bevels were taken. These were marked on the straight top edge of the pattern board for later transference to the timber. The board-to-keel angle was then marked and the board removed and cut to lines to guarantee a close fit. Each timber was cut to the pattern with the minimum bevel of those marked for each side, the sides beveled, top trimmed, and—once trimmed to fit perfectly—bedded and fastened in place."

The method seemed clear enough, but the execution was quite a challenge to inexperienced hands. Joe wrote:

"Donn, Mark, and I were bumbling along quite slowly and painfully, trying to get those devils to fit right on the frames. We had the right idea, but spent many, many hours whittling end grain. For some reason, we waited to ask Dave to show us to do it until our fingers were bloody and our souls weary.

" 'Hey, Dave, why don't you do one so we can see how the masters do it.'

" 'Oh, I'll do it, but it's been a long time, so don't expect anything great.'

" 'OK, Dave, go to it.'

"The first thing we did was pick the hardest floor timber in the boat for him: 'Here is one, Do this.' I elbowed Donn in the ribs. It was the one right up next to the stern deadwood, the most vertical height and therefore the most end grain, with wicked bevels and a reverse in the frame to boot.

"The whole shop was watching as Dave climbed into the boat. . . . He seemed to be doing what we were doing, but there was something different. His pencils were stubbier, yet his moves were clean, exacting, and very deliberate. All bevels were put on the pattern piece and the pattern laid on the yellow pine and traced out. . . .

"Now to the bandsaw and zip, zip. Dave turned the table as the timber moved slowly through the different bevels. We were all amazed how gracefully this was done. A quick trip to the bench, a few shots with the spokeshave, and Dave marched to the whaler, leaving a trail of bewildered apprentices.

" 'No way,' I thought. 'He did it much too fast. Boy, is he going to have a lot of end grain to shave.'

"Well, that's the story—Mr. Foster slid the timber into place and called for a hammer. One light, well-placed TUNK, and squeak—solid as a rock on all sides and bottom. A perfect fit.

"We all go nuts. Dave laughs and goes home to lunch.

"None of the three of us ever managed even close to this performance, but the process we watched helped us to get better and better until we all were pleased in the end with the floor timbers."

* * *

It would not be right to leave the impression that the apprentices followed traditional practice to the letter. For one thing, stringers were added, something rarely found in old whalers. Still more of the railroad-building yellow pine was reused, with pieces scarfed together. "Between planing, cutting, and scarfing, with good bronze bolts, a few hours went into these beauties before they could be popped in," Joe wrote.

"Popped is the word—or, rather, BOOM!

"As we snugged the stringers into place, you could feel the tension was too great. But we were optimistic, and inexperienced. A few early warning cracks went unheeded. Suddenly, shop visitors were treated to a roar of splintering yellow pine.

"In my anguish, I heard a lady exclaiming to her friends: 'Wow! Look how they did that!'

"I glowered at the seeming sarcasm before I realized she really thought it was planned.

"For my part, it turned out to be a great good fortune. I got a feeling for yellow pine that has extended far beyond that experience. . . ."

A switch to white oak, scarfed at the bench but joined in the boat, solved the problem of fitting stringers to the difficult turns of the whaler's bilges.

* * *

Caulking the hull with cotton.

Fastening a bilge stringer in place.

Master Builder Foster shows how it is done.

The hull nears completion as thwarts and
coamings are fitted.

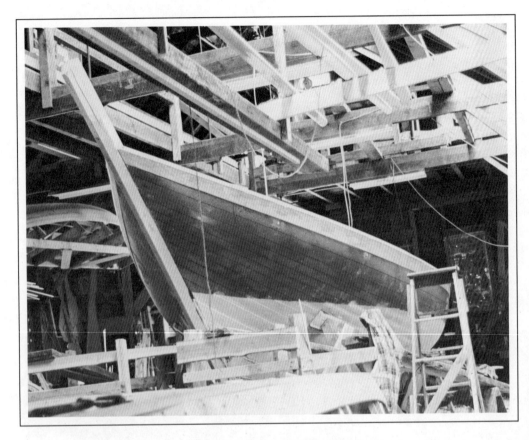

Almost ready to leave the shop.

Moving day.

There was one last departure from Tancook tradition when the deck was laid. Actually, the job was begun in the traditional way, laying 1x6 boards straight over the sheer strakes and then trimming them off. But the apprentices rebelled. "It was too easy," Dave Foster recalls. "It wasn't fancy enough for them, and they wanted to learn how to do a yacht-type deck such as we put on other boats. We used the cedar we had set aside for the decks for floorboards instead, and got some clear pine, about an inch thick and half an inch wide. They laid it down in a herringbone pattern, with no king plank. It worked out real well."

5 A Rig "Simple and Powerful"

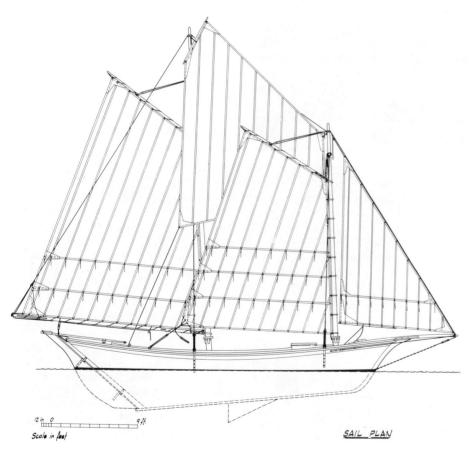

12 in 0   9 ft.
Scale in feet

SAIL PLAN

Howard Chapelle prepared a sail plan for the Middle River boat from old photographs and with help from a sailmaker, probably Randolph Stevens, Amos's son and David's father. Chapelle wrote:

"The rig was the old pilot-schooner with a long pole mainmast head in lieu of a top mainmast. The whole rig was simple and powerful; the boat was worked in strong winds under foresail alone, or under full mainsail and jib. If these changes in area showed too much sail, in either case, she was reefed. The rig was supplemented in light weather by a pilot-boat main staysail, now called the 'fisherman staysail.' The working rig was not a small one by today's standards, and this gave sufficient sail for work in moderate weather without necessitating use of light sails. By keeping the height of the rig moderate, it could be carried longer without reducing sail. . . . The only objection to the whaler rig that I ever heard of on Tancook Island was that the foresail sheet was hard to flatten in a breeze without luffing, owing to the powerful lug-foresail."

In preparing a sail plan for the Apprenticeshop's whaler, the builders merely reduced Chapelle's dimensions, cutting the sail area uniformly by 14 percent. Mark Swanson used Skene's *Elements of Yacht Design* for guidance in calculating spar scantlings. This resulted in a mainmast that was 35'4-1/4" overall, 5-1/2" diameter at the partners and 2-3/4" at the masthead, and a foremast of 25'4" overall, 4-1/8" at the partners and 2" at the masthead. The spars were of spruce cut on a Sheepscot farm not far from where local lore has it that spars were cut for the USS *Constitution*.

Roughing out the spruce spars with a chainsaw.

Next, a broadaxe is used to shape the spars.

A lipped adze is used to shape the spars.

tive anchoring for the shrouds. Asked whether they had deadeyes or lanyards, Mason replied:

"No, they just had thimbles. Years ago, they didn't even have chainplates. They just had a big eye like you would put in the mast. The blacksmith would make what they called an eyebolt. That would go right down and pin under the thwart. They'd have a hole in the end of the bolt and they'd put on a washer or two and just drive a pin through —a nail or something—so it wouldn't fall out. . . .

"They came up with a square link in it, and you reeved your lanyard through that and through the thimble that was spliced in the rigging. You just reeved through both of them and hauled her down so you had enough turns on so the thimble was pretty well filled up."

When he sailed the Apprenticeshop's whaler at the time of her maiden voyage to Mahone Bay, Mason remarked that her spars appeared about as heavy as those of the old-timers, her masts a little heavier aloft. "Years ago, the old mainmast would just bend the top like a whip handle," he recalled. "As you were sailing along, you would see the topmast just bending ahead. They didn't lose many, though. They were just growing sticks and they'd bend a lot before they'd break. Probably the rigging would give way, or something like that."

Still, the Apprenticeshop builders decided to play it safe. Running backstays helped to bring peace of mind to crews in heavy going, but, even so, when running before the wind in a real blow the mainmast takes on a decided "S" shape where pressure is exerted by the gaff.

* * *

Nat Wilson cut the sails in the traditional vertical style, using #10 duck for the fore and main, thirteen-ounce army duck for the jib, and a light Egyptian cotton for the staysail. One Tancook tradition that was not necessary for Wilson to emulate was cutting the sails on ice. Joseph Pearl's sail loft on the island had not been large enough to lay out sails the size of those required for whalers, but there was a pond two or three hundred yards away. Perry Stevens recalled that "he used to go down and lay off his sails, drive nails in the ice the shape of his sails, and then he laid the cloth and cut them up. . . . Very often he would get me to help him cut the sails down on the ice. For cutting a small sail I'd get 15 cents, and for a large sail 25 cents."

Rope stropped blocks for the running rigging.

Although the earliest Tancook whalers had rope shrouds, the Apprenticeshop's whaler followed later Tancook practice in having single galvanized wire shrouds, with no spreaders. On the advice of Nat Wilson, the East Boothbay sailmaker, 5/16" 7x7 wire was used. With an eye to tradition, turnbuckles were rejected in favor of lignum vitae deadeyes. The earliest whalers, according to Tom Mason, had an even more primi-

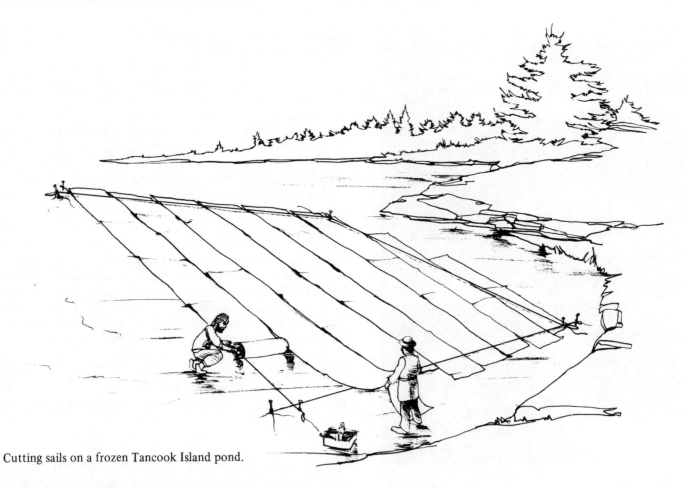

Cutting sails on a frozen Tancook Island pond.

Wilson strongly advised against using the traditional club on the big overlapping foresail, although he agreed that a club would help achieve optimum set for this powerful driving sail. "I thought it would be a killer," said Wilson, essentially reiterating a longstanding apprehension. E.A. Fader, the Mahone Bay skipper quoted earlier, said this about the old-time foresail:

"It sheeted way back of the mainmast to the standing room (the cockpit, as it is now called), had a heavy hardwood club with iron strap where the sheets hooked. In tacking, one man caught that club under his arm and walked around the mainmast and hooked the sheet on the other side. Woe betide you if you lost your hold on that club. If there was a good breeze you were liable to get your ribs or your head cracked, but they sure were a driving sail."

At first, the Apprenticeshop crew was seduced by tradition into including a two-foot foresail club. But experience quickly taught them that Nat Wilson had been right: this was one link with the past best done without.

* * *

The Tancook whaler emerges from the shop ready for launching.

Dave Foster and crew rig the whaler.

As eyewitnesses such as Fader and Edwin Pugsley noted, most of the old whalers had tanned sails to inhibit mildew, and in rain or fog the drippings were messy, to say the least. Fader reported that the preservative was made "by boiling spruce bark and rigging tar and some logwood bark." Nat Wilson of course had access to modern chemical preservatives, in this case a mildew-inhibitor called Canvak. This does not notably affect the original white color of sails, although after periodic treatment those of the Apprenticeshop's whaler tended to turn grayish.

Halyards were dacron, mostly 7/16", some larger. A try was made at giving them a more traditional look by treating with pine tar, but most of that washed away fairly quickly as sailing time began to add up. And sailing time began in mid-1979 when—after a year and a half—the Apprenticeshop's Tancook whaler was launched as the *Vernon Langille*.

6 Home to Tancook

The launch of the *Vernon Langille,* at the Burgess Marina on the Kennebec on July 7, 1979, was carried out in traditional Bath fashion —that is, she was fully rigged and ballasted (310 twenty-pound pigs), and she was decked from the tip of her bowsprit to mastheads to the end of her main boom with signal flags. The flags were provided by G. Baer Connard, a retired BIW executive who advised on launching protocol. Mrs. Howard I. Chapelle of Camden, widow of the man who had done most to preserve the lines of such traditional craft—not to say the very lines from which the *Langille* was adapted—did the christening, cheered on by an appreciative crowd of Museum officials, trustees, apprentices, and enthusiasts.

Master Builder Dave Foster, eager to try the *Langille* out, quickly mustered a crew to sail her to the Apprenticeshop's float, two miles upriver. Light, flukey winds made it necessary to row most of the way, however, and Foster had little chance to test her sailing qualities that day. He did note with satisfaction that she ghosted along nicely in the faintest breeze.

A week later, Foster and an apprentice crew sailed the *Langille* to Vinalhaven, fifty miles down the coast and the point of departure for her impending voyage to Nova Scotia. En route Foster put in at East Boothbay for a short shakedown with Nat Wilson. Wilson, like Foster, was pleased with the performance in light to moderate airs.

"When you build a boat, you begin to get expectations about how she will perform," Foster said. "Often you are disappointed, but not with this boat."

Launch day. The *Vernon Langille* approaches the dock after a successful launching.

87

The *Vernon Langille* leaves hardly any wake.

Start her sheets a little and she responds like a thoroughbred.

* * *

The dream of sailing a Tancook whaler "home" to Tancook Island had its inception the moment the first timber was cut for the keel of the (not yet named) *Vernon Langille*. Everyone from the Apprenticeshop wanted to share her with the old-time boatbuilders and fishermen who had encouraged the project. And, as David Stevens had suspected, they aimed to enter the International Schooner Races starting July 26 at Hubbards in St. Margarets Bay.

On July 21, two weeks after her launch, the *Langille* drifted with the ebb tide out of Hurricane Sound, all sails set. Lance Lee was in command of a crew of six. There was Steve Bailey, a former sailing instructor at the Outward Bound School on Hurricane Island, who served as navigator on the initial crossing of the Bay of Fundy, then took command for the return voyage and remained skipper for the next two years. And there was Joe Postich, first mate, and his fellow builder, Donn Costanzo, along with apprentices George Westbrook and John Stenquist.

For this first voyage, the *Langille* towed a nine-foot, apprentice-built Norwegian pram and carried an eight-man Avon life raft. In addition to Stearn's Deliverance-type work-vests, worn when under way, there were Class 1 PFDs for all hands. Equipment included a six-inch Ritchie flat-card compass and a "hockey puck" hand-bearing compass, plus a portable direction-finder which Bailey indicated could give a fix within about ten miles of true position.

As for the *Langille*'s full complement of equipment, let us turn to the briefing subsequently developed by Steve Bailey, as taped aboard the *Langille* preparatory to a later voyage. Bailey begins forward:

"On the foredeck we have two anchors always rigged and ready—a 40-pound Danforth on the starboard side and a 50-pound stock anchor on the port side. These are your emergency brakes. You want them rigged and ready to go at a moment's notice, with their rodes flaked down.

"The Danforth rode leads through a little metal fitting you see on the foredeck here. The line is just pushed through the hole into the little bulkhead that's just forward of the foremast, so if you let go for some unexpected reason the line isn't going to be lost. It's important to remember that nothing goes on top of the line . . . because that line has

to be clear to run free when you want it. If there's anything on top of it, it's guaranteed to be jammed inside.

"The stock anchor is flaked just forward of the cuddy hatch here. That's ready to go, too. If you try to take a line from a coiled position, it's always going to end up in a pile of spaghetti, but if you flake it down on deck it works just fine. The end of this rope also is tied to the mast up here at deck level.

"Coming off the foredeck into the cuddy, you'll find there are two nets on either side. The portside net is a catch-all closet. You'll find spare propane tanks and freon tanks, spare batteries, spare canvas and gloves. . . . The fog bell is located over there on that port side.

"In the starboard net is the emergency stuff you want to be able to get at in a hurry: foghorns—a mouth foghorn and a freon foghorn; flashlights, from a beam gun to a red lens flashlight and a white lens flashlight. . . .

"Just forward of the cuddy hatch ports are four small green metal boxes, marked for tools, rigging, first aid, and flares. . . . The flare box has aerial flares, parachute flares, hand-held flares, and a large orange square. . . .

"Coming a little further aft, on this bulkhead here on the backside of the cuddy are five lanyards, and on those are hung the dock lines and the towing line. . . . In the cuddy again, the VHF radio is on the starboard side as you enter. It is also our weather pickup. Beneath it is the fire extinguisher.

"A little more aft, we've got fenders stowed up on the port side. That plastic bucket is our substitute for the classic cedar bucket, the head. Another bucket is filled with rope and marlin, odds and ends when you need a scrap of line.

"Amidships is a gray case that has running tackle on top of it. That's the centerboard trunk. Inside is the centerboard, a sheet of stainless steel—somewhat exotic for such a fishing boat. It weighs about 300 pounds and runs up and down on that tackle. . . .

"Stowed on either side of the cockpit are ten-foot oars. On the starboard side, I like to keep my boathook. On the port side is the fenderboard. . . . A little further aft, the life raft. . . . This vessel is fitted with enough flotation so that, even full of water, it will float. . . . Probably the safest thing in most cases is to stay with the boat. But if the boat capsizes it might be a good idea to have a life raft standing by alongside.

Close-hauled, the *Langille* heels and shows her graceful underbody.

This is a $3,000 piece of gear. . . . That's why it has a crate to protect it.

"Coming a little further aft in the cockpit here, on the port side is a bilge pump made out of PVC. . . . The leadline is stowed over here between the knees in the main thwart. . . . The nets back here in the cockpit are for navigational equipment, horns, lights.

"Aft of the helmsman, just underneath the after deck, is a life ring. . . . Also back in here on the port side is a EPIRB (emergency position-indicating radio beacon), used for conditions where you might have to exit the vessel. . . .

"The 12-volt batteries for the VHF and the running-light system are underneath the floorboards in the cuddy. The stove is a two-burner propane. . . . Fishing gear is kept underneath the lazarette here—two handlines, a spool of codline, and about 150 extra hooks. . . ."

* * *

It was altogether fitting that a standard briefing should conclude with an enumeration of fishing gear, for, even though the *Langille* had to stow too much gear to allow for fish holds, the Tancook whaler was after all a fishing vessel and had been designed for that purpose in the place where they were now headed. As departure had been delayed for a full day by fog, and the crew had every intent of competing in the International Schooner Races at Hubbards on the 26th, they decided to sail directly across the mouth of the Bay of Fundy—120 miles of open water—rather than take the more conservative heading by way of Cutler, the northern end of Grand Manan, and Digby.

The first morning was spent drifting and rowing, making a knot or two in calm seas with six oars. With a breath of air the *Langille* ghosted along nicely, and when the afternoon breeze came in from the southwest she was soon making five knots in a fifteen-knot wind.

By late afternoon of the 22nd the RDF indicated a position forty-five miles southwest of Seal Island, and dawn of the 23rd found the *Langille* a few miles SSW of Cape Roseway, across the Bay of Fundy and in the lee of Nova Scotia. The log recorded at 9:45 A.M.: "Two humpback whales sighted; also porpoise feeding on schools of herring and pollock that surround us in smooth sailing sea. Best of all, a horn, Gull Rock, and then the fog lifted and we caught our first sight of Nova Scotia."

The double-ended hull rows as easily as it sails.

* * *

While all hands had been to sea before, and both skipper and first mate had extensive open-boat experience, the *Langille* was new and untried. And even though the design had been developed for this very coast, few centerboard Tancook whalers had been sailed in recent memory, and a lot remained to be learned about the *Langille*'s capabilities when pressed.

"Already I could see a few rigging changes I would make," wrote Bailey. "The two-foot club on the clew of the foresail had to go. No doubt it helped to flatten the leach and make the sail set better, but the added efficiency was not worth the continual danger of someone being struck by that flailing stick when she went about. A simple lacing through the grommets would do just fine. . . ."

On the 24th, in a calm afternoon sea, George dropped a cod jig over the side, and in the next three-and-a-half hours thirty-one cod were landed and dressed. At dawn of the 25th, the crew rowed into Port Mouton to clear customs, but were advised to complete formalities at Liverpool—where the fish could also be sold. Bailey recorded: "We set off for Liverpool under oars, then picked up an afternoon breeze around 2:30 and sailed past Western Head, through the many gillnets of the Mersey River, and out to the government docks by the fish plant. . . . I spoke with the fish plant operator. It seems we should have saved ourselves the trouble of cleaning the fish, as they offered a high price for fish in the round. The cod weighted out at 78 lbs. and brought $18.75 in Canadian dollars."

With satisfaction Bailey concluded his entry: "We were now a commercial vessel."

* * *

Most of the 26th was spent rowing, with a modest boost from a light southwest wind in the later afternoon. The crew felt a growing frustration at the lack of wind, as the three-day schooner races were already beginning at Hubbards. Finally they put in at Middle Island near Lunenburg for dinner with Simon Watts, who owned the last of the sailing Bush Island boats, a smaller cousin of the Tancook whaler.

Simon joined the crew as the *Langille* sailed on towards Hubbards at dawn in a gathering onshore breeze. At 11:00 A.M. they were off the

During the trip to Nova Scotia the *Langille*'s fishing qualities were tested.

Lunenburg whistle buoy in thick fog, averaging three knots. The wind picked up, but the fog persisted. At 2:00 P.M. someone wrote in the log: "Misplaced geographically."

After an hour of circling and searching, they finally picked up a bell buoy which guided them into Hubbards in time to share cocktails with crew from a fleet of nineteen schooners, just in from their second day of racing. Within minutes there were more than twenty guests aboard, Nova Scotians admiring a vessel that recaptured a page from their history. The *Langille* was made an honorary member of the International Schooner Association on the spot.

There was terribly sad news, however. The Nova Scotians reported that Vernon Langille had died two weeks earlier.

* * *

On the third and final day of the races, the stiffest winds the *Langille* had encountered provided an exhilarating test against the other schooners. Beating to the windward in fifteen to twenty knots on the first leg, she overhauled several larger vessels and rounded the mark eighth in the fleet, and she held that position right down to the finish line in rising winds that forced the crew to reef both the main and foresail and to haul down the fisherman during a wild final downwind run. Even with shortened sail, she boomed home at over six knots.

On the 29th, it was on to Tancook in bright sunlight. Close ahead lay the island—open fields and pasture, spruce forest, rocky headlands. Steve Bailey wrote, "We might have imagined ourselves returning from Halifax in 1879, having sold a load of fish. . . .

"Tancook is still a working village, although many of the homes have been purchased by summer people and many of the old boatbuilding and fishing families have moved to the mainland. A few people drifted down to the dock to ask what we were about. Some seemed more interested in the Norwegian pram we had as a tender than in the whaler. Although we didn't have to scratch too hard to find old-timers who recalled what the Tancook whaler had meant to this island, most of the younger people knew little or nothing about them. It has been at least 30 years since the last of the hulks of the original whalers rotted away on the beaches. . . ."

After a visit with Pearly and Sarah Cross on the northwest end of the island, Lee and his crew set sail in a light southwest breeze for Indian

Port tack on a blustery day.

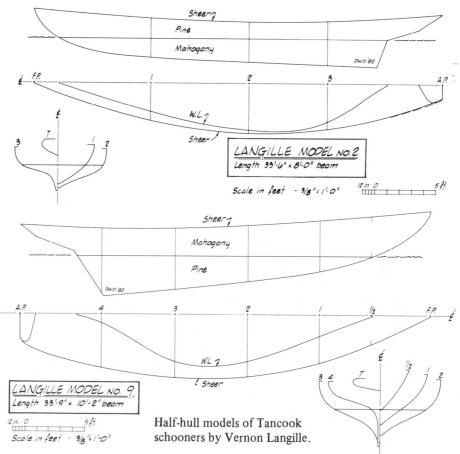

LANGILLE MODEL NO. 2
Length 33'-6" × 8'-0" beam

Scale in feet · 3/8" = 1'-0"

LANGILLE MODEL NO. 9
Length 33'-9" × 10'-2" beam

Scale in feet · 3/8" = 1'-0"

Half-hull models of Tancook
schooners by Vernon Langille.

Point to visit Vernon Langille's son, Cecil. The fog lifted and the day
became clear and warm, but the wind dropped, and the *Langille* was
making only three knots when an inboard skiff hailed. It was Cecil
Langille, who came on board for a sail before towing the whaler into
Indian Point.

Vernon Langille's shop looked as though he had just finished a boat
and was about to begin another. Joe Postich recalled visiting two years
before and felt deep distress that Vernon had not lived to see the
Vernon Langille. Donn Costanzo spoke feelingly of how much he had
looked forward to meeting Vernon. The visit was an act of homage. Be-

All sails set, the *Langille* ghosts along on a silver sea.

fore the whaler left Indian Point, Cecil entrusted Lance Lee with Vernon's precious collection of half-hulls, and Lee promised to return them after taking off the lines. There were also visits to Tom Mason and David Stevens, both of whom sailed the *Langille*.

* * *

The windward beat back to Maine was made via the coast, anchoring each evening. On August 8, the *Langille* rounded the corner of Cape Sable, and from there on it was a beam reach. With the winds rising to twenty knots, she made a consistent six to seven knots throughout the morning. The final cruise from Hurricane Sound to Bath was a relaxed one and arrival at home on the 18th coincided with festivities for the Maine Maritime Museum's Members' Day. As Dave Foster took Museum members on short sails out on the Kennebec, Steve Bailey recorded a brief entry on the *Vernon Langille:*

"She was a magnificent sight. Less than six weeks after her launching, she had already logged more than 600 miles at sea. She was all we had hoped. . . ."

Traditional Skills and Community Values

The *Vernon Langille* was all that her builders had hoped for, and yet it remains to be explained (private enthusiasms aside) why the Museum's Apprenticeshop would have built her in the first place. Here we need to say something about the expanded roles assumed by history museums in recent years. In addition to such traditional functions as collecting, conserving, studying, and displaying artifacts, they have moved to preserve and interpret cultural expressions of a less tangible sort—occupations and activities that are often regionally or ethnically rooted, and whose substance often can be imparted best by the act of emulation. Crucial to this new departure has been the support of such funding agencies as the National Endowment for the Arts.

Programs on the order of the Maine Maritime Museum's Apprenticeshop have been established as formal educational institutions aimed at teaching what are essentially styles of craftsmanship. There are other traditional-boatbuilding programs, but what distinguishes the Apprenticeshop from others is the context within which it operates—a major maritime museum which affords the opportunity for students and teachers to study at first hand a collection of nearly one hundred well-documented traditional watercraft, and to draw upon a wealth of archival materials relating to the communities whence they have derived.

A key premise is that the assimilation of regional styles and values is essential to a full understanding of such artifacts as traditional watercraft. As a result of the accelerated pace of technological change, older modes of transmitting skills have been altered and many traditional techniques are being transformed altogether—for example, in the course of an interview for the Museum a Maine boatbuilder confessed how much easier it was to get his keels out of a can (of fiberglass resin) than out of a tree. Institutions such as the Maine Maritime Museum have come to realize that such transformations can impede the capacity to comprehend and the capability for interpreting cultural artifacts in terms of the environment in which they were generated. In the future, it may become impossible to explain the cultural context of certain artifacts without resorting to anthropological models.

Documentary evidence, both verbal and graphic, has been the conventional means for taking account of cultural context. Yet, as any craftsman will indicate, there are intangibles involved in the creation and use of material objects which defy description and may not even be observable. How many times have we heard such expressions as, "Well, it's hard to describe this process," or "I can't really explain how it's done. . . ." Beyond that, there are the negative effects of those transformations wrought by our technological society, and the Museum—still charged with its traditional educational and interpretive functions—has had to take steps to fend these off. One of its salient programmatic responses has been the Apprenticeshop, founded in 1972 to perpetuate the skills and values associated with the building and sailing of traditional wooden boats.

More than one hundred young men and women have served eighteen-month apprenticeships, and they have completed more than a hundred small craft. As the Apprenticeshop's goals are integral with those of the Museum itself, a number of those boats have been built for display or in the interests of building towards a comprehensive collection. Many traditional workboats have literally become extinct, or, even if available

Apprentices haul the *Langille* up for the season using a block and tackle, just
as it might have been done on Tancook Island at the turn of the century.

In the spring the masts are retrieved from storage.

An A-frame is raised.

The mainmast is hoisted on the A-frame . . .

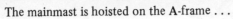

and set in place.

Transporting cordwood.

Delivering cordwood at Dix Island.

Unloading wood.

—or even if in the collection—are too deteriorated and frail to display usefully (i.e., in the water). Replicas are an obvious substitute, and here the dividends multiply. To make a replica for display, one first must learn something of how an original would have been built, and, while actually building, one learns much more. Under sail, much can be inferred about original performance. Matters of hull design, structure, and rig are clarified. With the *Vernon Langille,* for example, it immediately became clear that the foresail club—which enhanced the efficiency of the rig by helping to flatten the leach and make the sail set better—was not worth the risk of it hitting someone during a tack or jibe. This, in turn, revealed something about actual conditions aboard the original workboats, while also pointing up the impediments to faithfully replicating *everything* about a vessel such as the *Langille.*

Even when there is a historic original already in a museum's collection, restoration still may not be advisable, for in that process the patina, the evidence of a working life—something of the vessel's very essence—may be lost. Certain vessels ought simply to be stabilized, cradled, and stored for study. A replica will not evidence an in-service "history," but at least it can be displayed in its working milieu, in the water. Even when restoration of an original can be justified in terms of not compromising historic integrity, it may be infeasible financially. Often the cost of new construction is considerably less, all things considered, than the cost of extensively rebuilding an original.

More important, a reproduction can be a vital learning experience in terms of replicating technique. Ironically, even with the application of power machinery when none was available to traditional builders, a reproduction takes longer to construct. The *Vernon Langille* was lofted directly from the half-model, a method that would have been quick for a traditional builder of Tancook whalers, but took longer in the Apprenticeshop because of its unfamiliarity. In general terms, most vessels replicated outside of their traditional context are "one offs," whereas the old-time builders would likely have achieved a rhythm with numerous vessels on the same model. Patterns would have been developed and work-saving tricks devised as builders gained experience. As evidenced by the episode involving Dave Foster and the *Langille*'s floor timbers, real familiarity comes only with the refining of skills over a long period of time.

Replication entails many challenges. If the vessel is being produced from an old half-model, there are problems involving scale and the accuracy of developed lines, scantlings, the rig, and sail plans. Vessels such as the *Langille* are not usually built after some particular prototype but rather represent a synthesis of knowledge from various sources —plans, photographs, half-models, sometimes actual vessels, manuscript and printed descriptions, interviews with old-timers. Of course there are always questions that cannot be answered. How accurate is the available information? Are surviving models typical? Once the lines have been determined and the molds produced, there are other practical considerations. The original vessels might have used superior types of wood not readily available any more. What should be substituted? On the other hand, the originals might have been planned with an eye to a short working life, perhaps embodying materials that were economical and easily obtainable but susceptible to rot. For example, vessels built in Maine and the Canadian Maritimes often used birch and red oak rather than the more lasting white oak; in a replica, however, a long productive life is ordinarily an essential criterion for selecting materials.

Or take fastenings. In the mid-19th century Muntz metal was widely used, as were pure iron and iron alloys. None of these is readily available today, for demand has fallen below profitability as metallurgists developed broadly applicable alloys adaptable to boat building. The majority of Tancook whalers built in the latter 19th century were fastened with clenched iron boat nails, which accounts for the frames being wide and thin. Good iron clench nails being unavailable, the *Langille* was fastened with silicon-bronze screws; recall, however, that in retrospect Dave Foster thought copper rivets would have been preferable. Likewise, modern bedding compounds, preservatives, and paint, though maybe not "authentic," are desirable insofar as they can prolong the useful life of a replica and ease maintenance problems.

Quality and style in workmanship are major considerations when reproducing a vessel in a museum context. Traditional builders generally worked to tolerances appropriate to the intended use of a vessel, and a replica should approximate this practical approach. At the same time, it should not be forgotten that quality is inherent within the work performed, and that a builder's capabilities will be evident whether the product is a yacht or a workboat. Moreover, departures from the original can sometimes seem appropriate in terms of knowledge imparted to the builders; so it was with the *Langille*'s "yacht deck."

The *Langille* was generally masted and rigged in accord with traditional early-20th-century practices. But there were divergences dictated by her intended use in sail training, these including the substitution of wire standing rigging for rope and deadeyes and turnbuckles for eyebolts and thimbles with a lanyard reeved between; as mentioned before, the dangerous foresail club was removed after early trials. In the course of routine maintenance and fitting out, there were experiments with old techniques such as setting masts by means of a scissors derrick. Apprentices learned about procedures for hauling, about the knotwork used in handling and securing cargo. They found out that a boat the size of the *Langille* can be rowed with some degree of ease. The *Langille* became something of a laboratory for testing the potentials and constraints of working sail. Indeed, all the most valuable lessons center on *capabilities,* both of the vessel herself and of her crew.

* * *

In the years since 1979 the *Vernon Langille* has been used regularly in sail training programs, first by the Museum itself, then in conjunction with Tripmaster, Inc., and later with the WoodenBoat School, as the

Transporting sheep.

chusetts, and, nearer to home, the Windjammer Races on Penobscot Bay. Wherever she has gone, she has represented the Maine Maritime Museum, flying the flag of the Apprenticeshop program, and signaling its accomplishments in stimulating interest in traditional small craft, fostering the skills embodied in traditional building techniques, and imparting a sure knowledge of how to operate such craft safely and capably.

Among those who have become most familiar with the *Langille* over the years is Roger Taylor, author of the *Good Boats* series and president of International Marine Publishing Co. Taylor has immense regard for the Tancook whaler as a type, calling it "one of the greatest ever developed," and for the *Langille,* both as the most faithful extant embodiment of the type, and as an effective educational tool. In the latter regard it seems appropriate to recount a few observations, excerpted from an account published in the May-June 1984 issue of *WoodenBoat:*

"My own sailing in the *Vernon Langille* has mostly been when using her as a schoolship to teach the WoodenBoat School's course in the elements of seamanship. She attracts students who recognize a rather rare opportunity to sail in a replica of a traditional vessel unadulterated with contrivances of the mechanical—not to say electronic—era that usually seem to find their way on board for "practical" reasons. The *Vernon Langille* has no diesel engine hidden in the bilge (Tancook whalers don't have enough bilge for such shenanigans anyway) and no electronic sounding device or digital-reading speedometer piercing her pristine skin. I realize such contrivances can contribute to a vessel's safety—if you're always ready for their demise—but I think it's really better to leave them out of schoolships. On the first course I taught we inherited a radio with the vessel and dutifully listened to the weather 'forecast' every morning. On the second course we left the radio ashore, but I brought on board a barometer. Now, rather than listen to a voice talk to us from a faraway room with no windows, we had to actually look at the sky in our immediate vicinity, tap the glass (we almost wore it out with tapping) and actually *think* about what the weather might do, rather than just listen and believe. We did at least as well at not being surprised by the weather as did the radio broadcaster. . . .

"We start school by going over the vessel in some detail, naming everything in sight and learning what all the various pieces of running rigging do. Despite the apparent complexities of what is to most students an unfamiliar rig, we've had our hands on every bit and piece

Museum has sought to maximize the vessel's potentials in imparting seamanship. With a crew of six students under an experienced captain and mate, she has ranged from Mahone Bay to Cape Cod and Newport, and she has carried cargoes as diverse as granite, sheep, cranberries, cordwood, woodstoves, and fiberglass resin. She has participated in the International Schooner Races in Nova Scotia, Operation Sail '80 in Massa-

The tiller comb provides the helmsman with a rest.

Rowing in a calm sea.

Vernon Langille leads the Camden-Rockland schooner fleet at the start of a race.

So easily is a Tancook's hull driven that it will ghost along on a breath.

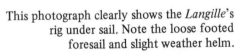

Transporting granite.

This photograph clearly shows the *Langille*'s
rig under sail. Note the loose footed
foresail and slight weather helm.

within an hour. I was intrigued to discover that going through this identical process on an 'efficient' marconi-rigged cruising ketch equipped with many 'labor-saving' devices took four hours. . . .

"For the first couple of days, the students don't know quite what to make of the *Vernon Langille* with her throat and peak halyards on the foresail and mainsail, her long, overhanging main boom, her big centerboard, her rows of reef points, her bowsprit, her foresail that needs tending like a jib when you tack, and her club-footed jib that doesn't. But then they get used to this paraphernalia, find that once understood it works in a straightforward manner, and realize that a vessel they originally thought was complicated is really very easy to sail. Usually, sometime on the third day, somebody sits back, looks around, and says 'Why wouldn't this be an ideal boat?' "

Why not, indeed? Certainly it has been close to an ideal vehicle for expanding the horizons of the Maine Maritime Museum. As outlined in the initial proposal submitted to the National Endowment for the Arts, the Tancook project aimed "to 'recapture' and record" a type of Northeast-coast workboat that was all but extinct. Subsequently the Tancook whaler became a living, working exhibit for the Museum, and it helped catalyze a more active role for the Museum in documenting and building historic small craft. The *Vernon Langille,* then, furthered some of the best aspects of traditional museology, but it has done much more, impelling the Maine Maritime Museum in new directions which have strengthened its understanding of community dynamics, enhanced its sensitivity to cultural context, and provided a touchstone for the interpretation of maritime history within its essential social matrix.

A Note on Sources

Fundamental to the construction of this narrative has been the series of taped interviews conducted on Tancook Island and elsewhere in the Mahone Bay region of Nova Scotia by an Apprenticeshop team in November 1977. Interviewees included Vernon Langille, Cecil Langille, Tom Mason, Pearly Cross, Mortimer Pelham, David Stevens, and Perry Stevens. The original tapes, along with transcriptions, are held in the archives of the Maine Maritime Museum (MMM) in Bath. A valuable supplement to these interviews is another series conducted by Kathy Kuusisto for the Explorations Program of the Canada Council in 1976 and quoted extensively in her two-part article, " 'It All Went With Our Living': Life Patterns of Tancook Families," in *The Occasional* (Nova Scotia Museum), vol. 4, no. 4 (Fall 1977): 32-37; and vol. 5, no. 1 (Spring 1978): 26-31.

Other primary documents, all held in the archives of the MMM, include accounts pertinent to building the *Vernon Langille* by David Foster, Mark Swanson, Joe Postich, and Donn Costanzo, and a synthesis drafted by Lance Lee. A manuscript transcription of a newspaper article, c1930, by E.A. Fader, "Reminiscence of an Old-Timer From Chester, Nova Scotia," is most illuminating, as is an untitled Tancook reminiscence, c1965, by Edwin Pugsley. There also are pertinent notes in the MMM archives from Dave Dillion and Steve Bailey, and correspondence from L.B. Jenson of Hubbards, Nova Scotia, and Kathy A. Moggridge (*née* Kuusisto) of Halifax.

For the history of Nova Scotia and specifically the Mahone Bay region, the essential starting points are Thomas Haliburton, *Historical and Statistical Account of Nova Scotia* (1829), and Mather Des Brisay, *History of the County of Lunenburg* (1870). Frank Parker Day's novel *Rockbound* (1928, reprint ed. 1973) depicts life on Ironbound Island (a neighbor of Tancook) in the early 20th century. One should also consult Thomas F. Knight, *Fishes and Fisheries of Nova Scotia* (1866-67), and George Brown Goode's encyclopedic *The Fisheries and Fishery Industries of the United States* (1884-87).

On the Tancook whaler, the pioneer published account is Ernest A. Bell, "The Passing of the Tancook Whaler," *Yachting,* February 1933, pp. 55-6+. Technical descriptions first appeared in Howard I. Chapelle's *American Small Sailing Craft: Their Design, Development, and Construction* (1951), published shortly after Chapelle's discovery of the Middle River boat, and in David Cabot, "The New England Double Enders," *American Neptune,* vol. 12 (April 1952), reprinted in *Thirty Years of the American Neptune,* ed. Ernest S. Dodge (1972). An interview with George Stadel (MMM archives) covers a range of topics pertinent both to Tancook whalers and to Tancook Island.

A wealth of information on whaler-type vessels built in the 1920s and 30s is contained in an interview with George Blenkhorn (MMM archives). Also useful is Ralph Wiley's autobiographical *Preacher's Son* (1972), and articles Wiley published in the June 1943 and June 1948 issues of *Yachting.* On whaler-type vessels built more recently on the West Coast and Gulf, see Diana Thompson, "British Columbian Prier Builds Tancook Whaler," and John Gardner, "Excellent Sailing Ability Claimed for Gaff-Rigged Tancook Whaler," both in the May 1977 issue of *National Fisherman.* For a splendid description of one of Peter Van Dine's fiberglass whalers, see Roger C. Taylor, "The Tancook Whaler *Nimbus:* Reminiscence of a Love Affair," *Small Boat Journal,* April/May 1983, pp. 70-75. Taylor's account of Wiley's *Mocking Bird* appears in the first volume of his *Good Boats* series (1977). With regard to the *Vernon Langille*, the article from which the lengthy quote at the end of the text was taken is "Sailing a Tancook Whaler," *WoodenBoat*, May-June 1984, pp. 82-87.

All unidentified photographs were taken by employees of the Maine Maritime Museum and are in the MMM archives.

Index

Page numbers in italics refer to illustrations.